Citizenship in Action

3

SARAH EDWARDS
ANDY GRIFFITH
MIKE MITCHELL
PETER NORTON
WILL ORD
CLARE RICKETTS
ANNE RILEY

Heinemann

Heinemann Educational Publishers
Halley Court, Jordan Hill, Oxford OX2 8EJ
Part of Harcourt Education

Heinemann is the registered trademark of
Harcourt Education Limited

© Sarah Edwards, Andy Griffith, Mike Mitchell, Peter Norton,
Will Ord, Clare Ricketts, Anne Riley, 2003

First published 2003

07 06 05 04 03
10 9 8 7 6 5 4 3 2 1

British Library Cataloguing in Publication Data is available
from the British Library on request.

ISBN 0 435 808044

Edited by Nicola Haisley
Produced by Wooden Ark Studio

Original illustrations © Harcourt Education Limited, 2003

Illustrated by Joan Corlass, Margaret Jones, Tony Richardson,
The Art Business
Cover design by Jonathan Williams
Printed and bound in China by Everbest

Cover photo: ©Still Pictures/Mark Edwards and Press Association

Acknowledgements
Every effort has been made to contact copyright holders of
material reproduced in this book. Any omissions will be rectified
in subsequent printings if notice is given to the publishers.

Make Votes Count logo on p10 reproduced with permission.
Cartoon on p51 ©Peter Brookes/The Times Newspapers Limited,
London (15 February 2001).
Article on p84 from
http://www.wotw.org.uk/showcase/brazil.html. Reproduced with
the kind permission of the British Council.

The publishers would like to thank the following for permission to
use photographs:
S R Greenhill/Richard Greenhill (left), Rex Features/Nils
Jorgensen (centre), Corbis/Gareth Brown (right) p.8; Topham
p.9; Photofusion/Molly Cooper (left), PA/J Green (right) p.11;
PA/J. Giles (top left), PA/J Green (top right), Rex Features/N.
Bailey (bottom left and right) p.13; Topham/PA (main photo),
PA (top), Peter Evans/Harcourt (bottom) p.16; PA (top), PA/M.
Stephens (bottom) p.17; Rex Features/Ray Tang p.18; PA/Stefan
Rousseau (left), Photofusion/Paula Solloway (right),
Photofusion/B Watkins (right) p.20; PA (top left), Rex
Features/Nils Jorgensen (top right), Gareth Boden (centre),
Photofusion/Peter Olive (bottom) p.22; Photofusion/Martin
Bond (left), Rex Features (centre), S R Greenhill/Richard
Greenhill (right) p.23; Mary Evans Library (top), PA/EPA
(bottom) p.24;Topham/Imageworks p.26; Still Pictures p.27;
Getty p.28; Topham/Imageworks p.29; PA (top), Alamy/David
Hoffman/Janine Weidel (bottom) p.31; Alamy/Robert Harding
(left), Photodisc (centre), Still Pictures/Fritz Polking (right) p.32;
Photodisc p.33; PA/F Hanson (top), Pete Morris (bottom) p.35;
Still Pictures/E. Duigenan/Christian Aid (left), Alamy/Bryan &
Cherry Alexander (right) p.36; Vin Mag Archive p.37; PA/EPA
p.38; PA/EPA p.39; AKG (left), PA/EPA (centre), Mary Evans
(right) p.40; Getty/Paul Avis (top); Alamy/Robert Harding
(centre), Alamy/Janine Weidel (left); Alamy/Brian Mitchell
(right) p.41; Topham/Imageworks (large); PA/EPA (small) p.42;
Rex Features/T. Kyriacou p.43; Panos/F. Hoogervorst p.45; Still
Pictures/Mark Edwards p.46-7; Still Pictures/Andrew Odum
(top left), Still Pictures/Ed Reschke (top right); Still Pictures/R.
Millet (bottom) p.47; Still Pictures/S. Vielmo p.48; Still
Pictures/Cytrynowicz/Christian Aid p.49; Still Pictures/Mark
Edwards (left), Rex Features/SIPA Press (right) p.50; Still
Pictures/Mark Edwards p.52; Topham/Imageworks (top), Panos
Pictures/J Miles (bottom) p.53; Still Pictures/D. Garcia p.54; Still
Pictures/E. Parker (top), Still Pictures/Mark Edwards (centre),
Still Pictures/Roland Seitre (bottom) p.55; Corbis/ M. Brennan
p.56; Corbis/Hulton p.57; Rueters/Sara Schwittek (top); Rex
Features/PCA (centre/left), Topham/Imageworks (centre/top),
Photofusion/W. Powell (centre/right), PA/EPA (centre/bottom),
Vin Mag Archive (bottom/left), Rex Features (bottom/right)
p.58; Rex Features (top), Topham/Public Record Office p.60;
PA/Hayden West p.62; Corbis/Sygma p.64; Lonely Planet
Images p.66; Corbis/Dave Houser p.67; Corbis Sini Baldi p.68;
Associated Press p.70; PA/EPA p.71; Still Pictures/P.Pieterse
(top), Photofusion/Lisa Woollett (centre), Still Pictures S.
Vielmo (bottom) p.72; Rex Features (left and centre),
Alamy/LGPL/Andrew Lambert (right) p.73; Hilary Fletcher
(left), Topham/UPPA (top, right), Anthony Blake/S. Irvine
(bottom, right) p.76; Corbis/V. Moos p.82; Ivybridge School
p.84; Photofusion/Jacky Chapman p.86; S R Greenhill/Richard
Greenhill p.88; S R Greenhill/Sally Greenhill p.89; Oxfam
Cymru/Craig Owen (left), Photofusion/Jacky Chapman (right)
p.91; Photofusion/P. Baldesare p.92; Barclays New Future p.93.

Contents

Introduction

What is Citizenship?

'Citizenship Education is education for citizenship, behaving and acting as a citizen, therefore it is not just knowledge of citizenship and civil society. It also implies developing values, skills and understanding.' (Crick Report, 1998)

Citizenship is a new National Curriculum subject for students at Key Stages 3 and 4. The aim of the Citizenship Programme of Study that you will follow is that you will develop the knowledge and skills you will need in the twenty-first century to become an informed, active and responsible member of a local, national and global community. As well as appreciating your own needs, you will appreciate the needs and views of others.

Some schools may have a timetable period for Citizenship, but most students at Key Stage 3 will develop their Citizenship understanding in a range of different ways. This may include tutor time, PSHE work, as a part of other subjects, within organised events such as the School Council or in voluntary work in school or the local community.

As a part of your Citizenship programme you will be encouraged to participate and work with others, both at school and in the wider community. At the end of Key Stage 3 you will be assessed by your teachers, who will discuss your progress and involvement in the school's Citizenship programme.

Each of the *Citizenship in Action* student books has been designed to help you understand the key ideas. The books use case studies to help you to understand important Citizenship issues. The text is written to encourage you to react and contribute with your own ideas and thoughts. Each chapter includes key words and definitions. You should try to learn these words and use them in the activities you will carry out. Many of the activities can be completed alone or with in a group – you could even try them out at home! At the end of each chapter there is a review and reflect section which helps you to pull together the ideas that have been mentioned.

Chapter summaries

Chapter 1 - Government and elections
Why is government important? This chapter outlines why and how citizens are an integral part of the political process. Key questions are addressed such as 'what is democracy?', 'why don't more people participate?', 'what does government actually do?', 'how does it spend our money?' and 'how and why is government in the UK structured as it is?' The review section enables students to consider what life is like in an undemocratic society.

Chapter 2 - Britain – A diverse society
What do we mean by 'living in a diverse society'? This chapter addresses the issues of the various cultural and ethnic backgrounds of the people of the UK, using topics like food and language to help explain the issues. Over the centuries, the UK welcomed a wide range of people from all over the world, and this chapter discusses the reasons why people move from one country to another and the issues involved. This enables students to reflect on the nature of national identity and citizenship.

Chapter 3 - Global issues
We live in an increasingly interdependent world, where problems and issues in one country can have a profound effect on others. Decisions and actions by UK citizens can have a global impact, for example, by selecting one product rather than another or boycotting some products. By using the case study of the issues relating to the Amazon rainforest, students begin to appreciate the inter-

relationship between a range of conflicting interests i.e. environmentalists, native populations and those seeking economic development. Students are encouraged to understand the competing claims of the various groups. This case study enables students to reflect and discuss a multi-layered issue from a range of differing viewpoints.

Chapter 4 - What is conflict?

Why do conflicts occur? By using a broad range of examples students are introduced to the relationship of religion and conflict. The issue of conflict resolution is discussed. Students are encouraged to reflect upon the nature of conflict and develop ideas for conflict resolution.

Chapter 5 - School linking: an introduction

This chapter enables students to reflect on their own lives, school, community and country by developing links with other students and schools across the world. How would they describe their school and community to others? What criteria would they use when seeking a partner school? What information do they need to gather, to pass on to the link school? What would they like to know about the link country and school? How do you organize a link and perhaps establish a link day?

Chapter 6 - Reviewing your evidence – end of Key Stage 3 assessment

As this Key Stage 3 course draws to a close, the issue of assessment has to be addressed. Students will have been involved in a wide range of activities and assembled a vast range of materials and evidence. Through a series of exercises, students are encouraged to make judgements about their course and the material they have gathered. The use of the Portfolio of Evidence or the Progress File as a part of the assessment process is discussed. A number of the exercises like Event Organization could be used to run real events. The TRP for this book uses the concept of a Citizen's Passport for assessing and recording the entire Key Stage 3 course. It is suggested that this resource is introduced to students in Year 7.

Where do you stand now?

As you work through the chapters in the book and the activities you will take part in, think about the following questions:
- What do we mean by democracy?
- What makes a good citizen?
- How and why do global issues affect me?
- What are the benefits of learning about Citizenship to our families, the community and the world?

Chapter 1

Government and elections

In this unit you will be looking at how groups of people can make decisions. You will see how important it is to take part in the democratic process and how this can be done by voting. You will also study how the British system of government works. You will think about:

Learn about...

- The British democratic system.
- Ways of making decisions and voting systems.
- How political parties organize election campaigns.
- How national and local government is organized.
- How the government raises and spends money.

Getting technical

Government the group of people responsible for running a country and creating laws and policies.

Democratic something that has been chosen by the people of a country. A government can be democratic.

Autocratic something that is ruled over by one person, who has not been chosen by the people. A country can be autocratic.

What happens when the leader dies?

I want to be ruled by a group of people elected by the country's people.

We take a vote.

I want to be ruled by one wise person.

What's a vote?

What if I do not agree?

Activities

In pairs, list the disadvantages of the two systems of government being discussed above. One is democratic; one is autocratic. Share your ideas with the rest of the class.

How did the British system of government develop?

Today, Britain is a democracy. The country is ruled by a government that is elected by the people. This is not always how Britain has been governed. For hundreds of years Britain was a monarchy. This means that the country was ruled by the king or queen.

The following information shows some of the important steps in the development of democracy in Britain.

What is the role of the monarchy in today's government?

Today, the monarchy still exists in Britain. The head of the monarchy – the Queen – does not rule the country.

Constitutional monarchy

As a Constitutional Monarchy, the country is ruled, in the monarch's name, by an elected government. However the Monarch retains a number of important ceremonial functions,

- Appointment of The Prime Minister
- Dissolution of Parliament
- Opening Parliament

Date	Important step	Facts
1215	Magna Carta	The king's power was reduced when the barons forced him to consult them on matters such as taxes
1689	Bill of Rights	This bill limited the powers of the king and set up rule by Parliament
1848	Chartist Petition	This movement campaigned for political reform including votes for all men, voting by secret ballot and yearly elections to Parliament
1928	The Suffragettes	This movement campaigned for votes for all women, which were finally granted in 1928

Getting technical

Constitutional monarchy a monarch whose powers are limited by the country's constitution

Parliament the highest law making body in Britain, consisting of the monarch and the Houses of Commons and Lords.

Activities

1 Do some research about the monarchy in Britain today. Then read these statements and decide if they are true or false. Discuss your answers with the rest of the class.

- The monarch decides government policy. — True/False
- The monarch appoints the government. — True/False
- The monarch has regular meetings with the Prime Minister to discuss government policies. — True/False
- The monarch is the leader of the government. — True/False
- The monarch opens Parliament each year and sets out what the government is aiming to achieve. — True/False
- The monarch is head of the Commonwealth. — True/False

2 Discuss with your partner each of the following types of government, monarchy, democracy and autocracy. For each one write down one advantage and one disadvantage.

3 You might like to use a reference CD-ROM or the internet to find some more of the facts relating to the monarchy.

Extension Activity

4 In a group, discuss the following statement: 'The monarchy is outdated in modern Britain.' You may need to do some more research before the discussion. Discuss the information and decide whether you agree or disagree with the statement. Your group must be able to justify its decision.

How can groups of people make decisions?

There are many ways that groups of people can make decisions. The method used to reach a decision depends on the importance of the decision to be made. Look at the following images.

A

B

C

● Someone voting for Big Brother

What would you like as part of your school meals?

Surveys or questionnaires are often used to find out people's opinions. This helps groups to make the best decisions about the subject of the questionnaire. These decisions are based on the responses given. By using these responses, the wishes of the majority of people are taken into account.

The Happynosh school meals company is about to take over your school's canteen. Before it does, it wants to know what the pupils like to eat. In pairs, discuss how Happynosh could collect this information. Who should it ask? What questions would it ask?

Sorry, chips are off today.

Are there any chips?

Activities

On your own, decide your answers to these questions.

1. Should children be allowed to get a job at any age?

2. Should parents be able to smack their children?

3. Should schools set homework?

4. Should the police pick up pupils truanting from school?

Now compare your answers with a partner or group. Are they the same? Who is right and who is wrong? As a whole class, decide what the answers are. Do this by voting – how many 'yes' or 'no' answers does each question get? Is the class answer right or wrong?

Who would you like in government?

In British parliamentary elections the results are decided using a system called 'first past the post'. The candidate with the highest number of votes is declared the winner. Some people argue that this can often mean that the person elected does not represent the majority of the people who voted. This is because there may be more than two candidates. All the votes for the other candidates can add up to more than the winning candidate received.

● Newly selected MP celebrates

Look at the following results for the constituency of Kettering in the 2001 General Election.

Labour	24,034
Conservative	23,369
Liberal Democrat	5,469
UK Independence	665

Activities

1. Draw a bar chart of the results.

2. Which candidate got the highest number of votes?

3. Which candidate won the election?

4. Add up the votes that the other three candidates received in total. How many people did not vote for the winning candidate? Do you think this is fair? Explain your answer.

5. Did the winning candidate get the majority of all the votes cast?

What could be used instead of 'first past the post'?

For many years the Liberal Democrat Party and other organizations have argued that the electoral system in Britain should be changed. They say that the system should be based on 'proportional representation' and that this would make the elected British government truly represent the majority of people.

● Logo taken from www.makevotescount.org.uk

The problem is that there are a number of proportional representation systems. Which system should be used? Each of the systems has advantages and disadvantages. However, they all take into account the number of votes cast to all candidates and try to make sure that the chosen government represents as many people as possible.

Getting technical

Single transferable vote a form of proportional representation in which the voters rank the candidates. Where the candidate doesn't need the vote it can be transferred to the next ranked candidate.

Alternative vote a form of proportional representation in which the voters rank the candidates. A candidate getting over 50% of the votes wins the election, but if no one gets over 50% then the 2nd choices are considered.

Voting in Britain – when and why?

People in Britain can vote in many different elections. They can use their vote to elect parish councillors, local government councillors or members of Parliament. The people they elect will represent them. Voting is usually done in secret so that no one else can see your choice and force you to change it. This type of voting is done in polling stations using ballot papers and ballot boxes. But are people given the chance to vote on other issues?

The euro – let the people decide?

Britain is part of the European Union (EU). Many countries in the EU have changed their currency to euros. Britain has not changed its currency. Many people think the government should follow the rest of the EU and change to euros. Others think that Britain is better off sticking to pounds and pence. This sort of decision is usually made by the government. However, many people argue that the government should let the people of Britain decide by voting in a referendum. This is when political decisions are made by the public, not the government.

Getting technical

Polling station a building where voting takes place; often a town hall or similar.
Ballot paper a slip of paper used to vote, which has all the candidates' names and boxes to tick your choice.
Ballot box a sealed box into which voters place their votes.

● Votes being cast at a polling station.

Within the picture identify the following specific parts:

• the returning officer
• the voting booth
• the ballot box.

● Protesters demonstating to change to the euro.

● Protesters demonstrating to keep the pound.

Activities

1. What is the 'first past the post' system? Explain it in your own words.

2. What is different about 'proportional representation'?

3. Do you think that there should be a referendum on the euro? Explain your answer.

4. Hold a class referendum on the euro. What is the outcome?

Extension Activity

5. Hold a class discussion on this statement: 'It is time to change Britain's outdated first past the post voting system.'

6. Write out a questionnaire for the Happynosh school meals company to find out which foods the pupils of your school prefer.

7. Look at the image of a polling station on the opposite page. For each of the identified parts, explain how it helps to make the election fair.

How do political parties try to gain votes during election campaigns?

During a General Election the national political parties and their candidates try to attract attention from the national media and so get as much publicity as they can for themselves and their policies. Even during local by-elections the candidates will try to get media coverage by the local media and, if possible, even national media. During elections the politicians use a number of strategies to gain the media coverage they desire.

Firstly, they produce a manifesto containing their party's policies for the election, which it releases at a special media show where the leader and many other senior party members explain the policies contained in the manifesto.

The policies below were taken from the Labour Party Manifesto for the 2001 general election.

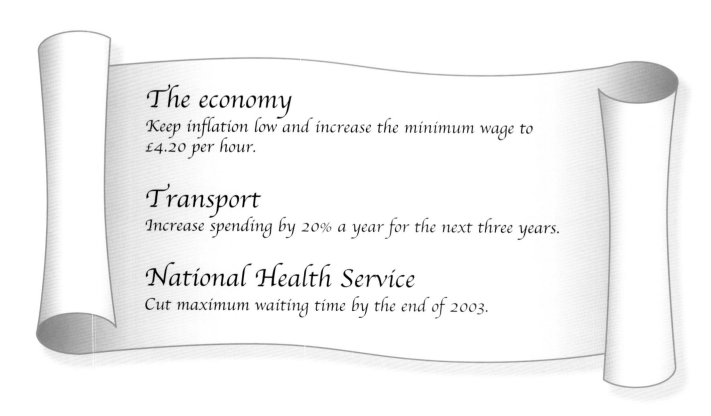

The economy
Keep inflation low and increase the minimum wage to £4.20 per hour.

Transport
Increase spending by 20% a year for the next three years.

National Health Service
Cut maximum waiting time by the end of 2003.

Secondly, the politicians use slogans to attract people's attention and to get ideas to stick in their minds. These are often unveiled in dramatic media styles using the sides of large lorries.

● Conservative poster

● Labour slogan unveiled by Tony Blair

The parties also use large posters around the country, which are unveiled in front of the press by a leading member of the party. These posters often concentrate on stressing the negative side of the other party's policies.

● Conservative poster

● Labour poster

Finally, the parties can make party election broadcasts. These are then shown on national television.

Why do some people not bother to vote?

My vote will not make any difference.

I'm too busy to vote.

We know who is going to win anyway.

I do not trust any of the parties.

In every election there are many people who do not vote. This could be for reasons like the ones on the left. Look at these statistics showing the percentage of people who voted in the last ten General Elections.

1966	76%
1970	72%
1974, Feb	79%
1974, Oct	73%
1979	76%
1983	73%
1987	75%
1992	78%
1997	71%
2001	59%

Because so many people are not voting in elections, many people are worried that the party that wins the election does not truly represent the British people. The following statistics show the percentage of the voters who voted for each of the three main parties in the last General Election.

Labour   41%
Conservative   32%
Liberal Democrat 18%

For this reason, politicians try hard to encourage everyone to vote, especially their supporters. Other people feel it is important for everyone to vote so that they can be sure that the party that wins the election does represent the opinion of the people of this country. Some people believe that it should be made illegal not to vote, as in other parts of the world. Others suggest that the way to get more people to vote is to make it easier to vote, for example, by introducing Internet voting.

Activities

1. Plot a bar graph of the percentages of people who voted.

2. In the 2001 General Election, what percentage of people did not vote?

3. What do you notice about the 2001 figure compared to the figures for the previous years?

4. Plot a bar graph of the percentages who voted for each party.

5. Which party got the largest amount of votes?

6. Did the party that won get the majority of the votes?

7. Does this party represent the majority of the voters?

Does age affect whether people vote?

Look at the following table showing the percentage of people of different ages who voted in the 2001 General Election.

Age group	Voted
18–24	38%
25–34	45%
35–64	62%

Activities

1 Plot a bar graph of the results. On the graph include a line to show the national average for the number of people who voted (59%).

2 In which age group did more than the average number vote?

3 In which group(s) did less than the average number vote?

4 In pairs, discuss the policies taken from the Labour Party manifesto (page 12).
   a What do they mean?
   b Why do you think they were included in the manifesto?

5 Look at the Internet and find the manifesto promises on the same areas for the other two main parties – Conservative and Liberal Democrat. Write these out.

6 Then look at all the statements and decide which party you agree with. Which one is it?

7 Hold a class election. Firstly, discuss which of each party's statements the class agrees with, and secondly, which party overall the class would vote for.

8 Look at the party slogans on page 13. What do you notice about them? Why do you think parties use slogans like these? Share your ideas with the rest of the class.

Extension Activity

9 Re-read the reasons given by people for not voting. What would you say to these people to try and get them to vote?

10 Discuss in pairs the following questions:
   a Why do you think some young people seem to have little interest in voting?
   b Why do you think so many older people vote?

11 Write a manifesto on issues that you think would encourage young people to vote.

How does Parliament work?

The British parliamentary system is based on two 'houses' –
the House of Commons and the House of Lords. Each plays
a different role in the setting of government policies.

● Inside the House of Lords

Speaker

Prime Minister

Leader of the opposition

Government benches

Back benches

Front benches

Opposition benches

Voting lobbies

● Inside the House of Commons

Members of Parliament are elected to the House of Commons by the public in General Elections. They are usually members of a political party. In Britain, the three main political parties are Labour, Conservative and Liberal Democrats.

The House of Lords was traditionally for Peers. These are people who have been given titles such as 'lord' or 'lady'. This may be for the work they have done in their lives while others may have inherited their title. The Peers can choose to represent a political party or they can choose to be independent.

Each year the parliamentary term starts with a state opening of Parliament in which the monarch reads a speech. This speech sets out the laws that the government intends to pass during the following year.

● State opening of parliament

How does the government work?

Once elected in the General Election, the government remains in power for up to five years. The government's term of office can end before the full five years is up if the political party that forms the government loses MPs. At this point, the government will call a General Election. It is the government's job to pass and amend laws according to the statements set out in their election manifesto. The role of the opposition parties is to support these laws if they feel it is in the country's best interest or to change or stop the changes to the law, if they feel it would not benefit the country.

● Tony Blair enters number 10 Downing Street after labour victory

How does a bill become law?

Changes to the law usually start as government 'bills'. A bill is a suggested or proposed law that has not yet been agreed by Parliament. It has to go through a number of stages before becoming law. Written below are the stages involved in the passage of a bill.

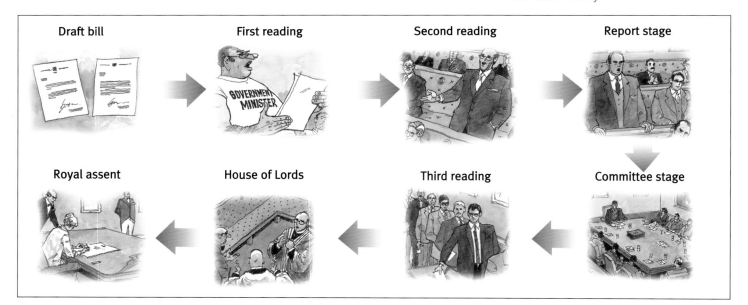

What is the role of cabinet?

To help with the running of the government, the Prime Minister appoints a cabinet. This is made up of ministers who are responsible for all the different areas of the government. Each minister is responsible for organizing the working of his/her department. To do this, the department is supported by a group of civil servants.

● Cabinet meeting

● Political campaigning

What is an MP's role?

Once a Member of Parliament (MP) has been elected, he/she must divide his/her time between the constituency they represent and the House of Commons. During the parliamentary sessions (see table 1a) an MP is expected to spend much of their time from Monday to Thursday around the Palace of Westminster or in the House of Commons so that if a vote is called they can be present. On Wednesdays, at 12 noon, most MPs like to be in the House of Commons, as this is Prime Minister's Question Time when MPs have the chance to question government decisions. Most MPs have to work long hours, not only attending debates in the House of Commons (see table 1b), but also reading their order papers that explain the business for the day in the House of Commons. In their constituency, the MPs hold regular surgeries where they meet with their constituents, even ones who did not vote for them, to discuss and offer help with problems they are having.

Getting technical

Constituency an area of a country that elects one representative to parliament.
Constituent a person living in a constituency who is entitled to vote in an election.

Table 1b Parliament Daily Working Hours

Monday	2.30pm to 10.30pm
Tuesday	11.30am to 7.30pm
Wednesday	11.30am to 7.30pm
Thursday	11.30am to 6pm
Friday*	9.30am to 3pm (selected dates only)

*There are also ten Fridays throughout the sessions when Parliament does not meet. During occasions of national importance, Parliament may also hold sessions at weekends.

Table 1a Parliament Calendar for 2002/03

Autumn Session
13 November to 19 December

Spring Session
7 January to 10 April

Half term break
13 February to 24 February (Constituency Week)

Summer Session
28 April to 17 July

Half term break (Called Whit Recess)
22 May to 3 June

What does the local council do?

Local councils are made up of councillors. They are elected in a similar way to Members of Parliament using a 'first past the post' voting system. Once all the councillors have been elected, the mayor is chosen. Councillors are not paid for their work, but they can claim back their expenses and get money for attending meetings.

As a member of the local council, I am responsible for helping to decide how to spend the council's £5.3 million budget. To do this, I am expected to attend regular council meetings to discuss and vote on the proposed actions the council is planning to take. I am also a member of two committees that are responsible for considering the spending in particular areas. I also need to keep in touch with the people in my ward, for which I arrange regular meetings (ward surgeries) where people can come and discuss their concerns.

Getting technical

Councillors elected members of the local council.
Ward an administrative division of a political constituency.

Activities

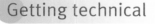

1. Use the information on pages 16–20, as well as your own research, to produce a pamphlet explaining to younger students how the British Parliamentary system works.

2. Discuss with a partner what you think the functions of the members of the cabinet might be. Share your ideas with the rest of the class.

3. Write a job description for an MP. Include what the MP does and what the MP's working times would be.

Extension Activity

4. Explain why most MPs are male and middle class. Think about issues like working conditions, hours worked, tradition and opportunity.

5. Make a note of the main stages that a government bill has to pass through. For each stage explain what has to happen.

6. Design a poster to advertise for a candidate to stand as a local councillor.

7. Use the Internet to find out more about your local council.
   a Who is the leader of the council?
   b What committees does the council have?
   c What does each committee do?

How does devolved government in Scotland, Wales and Northern Ireland work?

The government arranged for people in Scotland (September 1997), Northern Ireland (May 1998) and Wales (September 1997) to vote in a referendum. The people voted for power to be devolved, this meant that they wanted a separate form of government to run their areas. The Labour government then set up the Scottish Parliament and the Northern Ireland and Welsh Assemblies.

Scottish Parliament
The first full session of the Scottish Parliament took place on 12 May 1999. The Parliament is made up of 129 MSPs (Members of Scottish Parliament). Some of the areas of responsibility passed to the Scottish Parliament include social service, health, education, law and order and local government.

United Kingdom Parliament
All areas of the United Kingdom still elect a Member of Parliament to represent them. Parliament retains control of a number of responsibilities such as defence, foreign policy, immigration and employment.

Northern Ireland Assembly
The Good Friday Agreement recognizes the need for a separate Northern Ireland Assembly, made up of representatives elected by the people of Northern Ireland. The Assembly came into force on 2 December 1999 and is made up of 108 members. They are responsible for areas like education, environment, health and social services.

Finally, after a great deal of arguing between the political parties in Northern Ireland, devolution was suspended at midnight on Monday 14 October 2002.

Welsh Assembly
The first session of the Welsh Assembly was opened by the Queen on 26 May 1999. The Assembly is made up of 60 members who are responsible for areas such as education, environment, social services, transport and local government.

In Wales a 19 year old at work *does not* have to pay for a prescription.

In England a 19 year old at work *does* have to pay for a prescription.

Activities

1. In your group, pick one of the devolved governments and find out more about how it works. Prepare a talk to give to the rest of the class.

2. Which powers are common to all of these devolved governments? Which powers have been kept by the United Kingdom government?

3. If there are separate parliaments for Scotland, Wales and Ireland, some people suggest there should be an English Parliament. What reasons can you think of for an English Parliament? Discuss if you agree that England should have its own parliament.

Extension Activity

4. What is the difference between buying a prescription in Wales and in England? Use the Internet to find out more about this difference. You can also find out if there are other differences in law between the devolved sectors of the United Kingdom.
Discuss if you think this difference is fair

How does the government raise money?

The government needs to raise billions of pounds each year to pay for all the services it provides. This money is collected through taxes. The amount of tax paid to the government each year is set by the Chancellor of the Exchequer.

The following information shows the taxes paid by Mrs Singh through her monthly payslip. Her salary is £24,000.

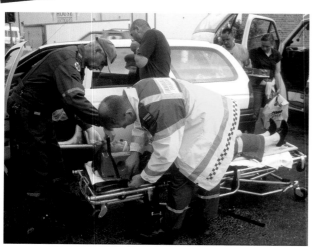

Pay Statement

Harcourt Education

Mrs Singh				004			1
				D Exact	461L		Monthly

PAYMENTS	HOURS	RATE		DEDUCTIONS		CUMULATIVE TOTS	
Basic Pay			2,000.00	Income tax	299.58	Gross	2,000.00
				National Ins.	150.99	Tax Gross	1,834.00
						Tax Paid	299.58
				Pension Monthy	166.00	Earn for NI	2,000.00
						NI ER	148.41
						NI EE	150.99
						Earn NI Co	
						EE NI Co	
						NI Rebate	
SMP						K Not Coll	0.00
SSP						Pension EE	166.00
				TOTAL DEDUCTIONS	616.57		
TOTAL PAY			2,000.00	NET PAY	1,383.43	PAY RECEIVABLE	1,383.43

Tax band	Percentage of income paid as tax	Income
Starting rate	10%	Up to £1960
Basic rate	22%	£1961 – £30,500
Higher rate	40%	Over £30,500

● Tax bands 2003

Income tax
This is paid by all people with a job. The amount paid is calculated by the Inland Revenue using the information in the table above.

National Insurance
This is also paid by all people with jobs, as a percentage of their wage, but it is also paid by the employer for each person they employ.

There are also a number of other forms of tax which are paid to the government (See opposite page).

- Armed forces.

- Repairs to local roads

- Other types of tax

- Refuse collection.

VAT Value Added Tax	Corporation Tax	Inheritance Tax
This is paid at 17.5% on most items people buy.	This is a tax on business profits. The amount of tax paid depends on the size of the business. Small – 19% Large – 30%	This is a tax on any money or belongings inherited from your relatives when they die. Everything over £250,000 is taxed at 40%

Activities

1 Using the table on the opposite page calculate approximately how much tax would be paid by the following people, then copy and complete the following table.

	Salary	Tax paid
Mr Jones	£10,000	
Mrs West	£20,000	
Mr Stewart	£100,000	

2 Plot a bar graph of each person's salary.

3 Why do some people pay more tax than others?

4 Do you agree that people who earn more should pay even more tax? Give reasons for your answers.

5 Think of all the things that the government and local councils provide. List these. Compare your list with the rest of the class and create a class list.

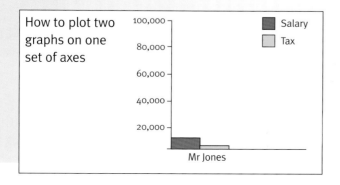

How to plot two graphs on one set of axes

Extension Activity

6 In groups, discuss the statement: 'Higher taxes are necessary to pay for the services we all need.'

7 National Insurance is used to pay for the National Health Service and pensions. If someone pays privately for these services, should they still have to pay National Insurance? Explain your answer.

8 The government is proposing to change the way local government is organized. Discuss these statements and decide if you agree or disagree with them. Be prepared to back up your decision with reasons.

- Local councils know best the needs of local people.
- Local councils should be given more power to run local services.
- Westminster should look after national concerns while local councils should look after all local issues.
- Unpaid councillors are not the best people to run the council.
- Local councillors should be paid a proper wage.
- Local people should elect the mayor, who should be paid to run the council.

Review and reflect

In this unit you have learned about the importance of taking part in the democratic process and about how democracy delivers fair and representative government for all the people of the United Kingdom.

Does democratic government always work?

Winston Churchill, Britain's leader during the Second World War, once said:

'Democracy is the worst form of government, except for the others.'

Discuss this statement. What do you think it means?

● Sir Winston Churchill.

Do countries always vote for the best leaders?

● Robert Mugabe.

One of the possible weaknesses of democracy is that the right of people to choose a government includes the right for them to make what the rest of the world might consider a bad choice. Throughout history there have been occasions when people have elected leaders who were not good leaders. In 1933 millions of German people voted for the Nazi Party led by Adolf Hitler. The Nazis were extreme racists and their actions resulted in the outbreak of the Second World War.

Democracy is often ignored by people in power. Read the following information about the election in Zimbabwe in 2002.

Mugabe wins 'rigged' Zimbabwe poll

Zimbabwe's President, Robert Mugabe, has won a fifth term in office. His party is accused of rigging the elections and using violence to make people vote for them.

Do the numbers of people who vote always mean the result reflects the wishes of the majority?

In the United Kingdom General Election of 2001, only 59 per cent of the population voted. This means that the government does not clearly represent the majority of the population. One of the suggestions to encourage people to vote in future elections was to change the ballot paper to include a vote for 'none of the above'.

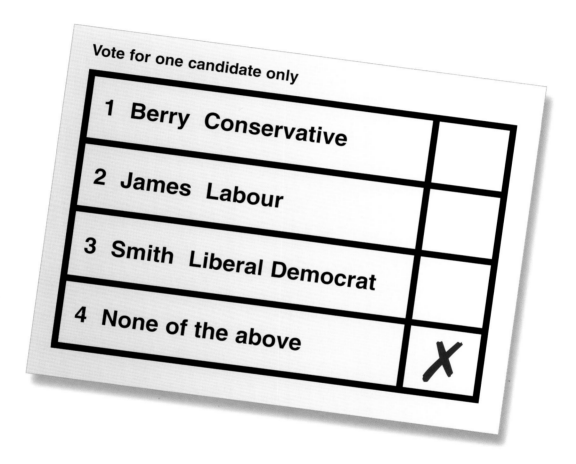

Vote for one candidate only

1 Berry Conservative	
2 James Labour	
3 Smith Liberal Democrat	
4 None of the above	X

Activities

1. With your partner, discuss how effective you think this 'none of the above' change to the voting system would be in getting people to vote.

2. How can people show they do not approve of any of the candidates in the present system?

3. What problems might there be if people were given the 'none of the above' choice?

Extension Activity

4. The government in South Africa during the twentieth century was not considered to be democratic. Find out why this was the case and what actions were taken against South Africa.

5. Use the Internet to find out why the recent election in Zimbabwe was considered not to be fair.

Chapter 2

Britain – A diverse society

Learn about...

- Our identities and the different national, religious, cultural, regional and ethnic identities.
- Why it is good to respect and appreciate diverse communities.
- How communities are interdependent around the world.

Remarkable Trees of the World – a book by Thomas Pakenham

Thomas Pakenham wrote a book about trees. The trees were from all over the world. The book took him four years to write. The heaviest and largest tree in the world is the sequoia from California. At 1500 tons, it is the largest single living thing in the world!

There are trees that animals rely on, such as the African baobabs, which elephants seem to worship.

The oldest living tree measured by scientists is a cone pine. It is also found in America, and is 4600 years old. The book also contains a photo of the 2200-year-old bo tree in Sri Lanka. This tree grew from a cutting from the original tree under which Buddha found enlightenment.

Getting technical

Sequoia a type of giant redwood tree found in North America.
Baobab a tropical African tree which has edible pulp.
Enlightenment discovery of the solution to problems of human suffering.

● African Baobab tree.

Activities

Diversity is something to be celebrated. It makes our lives feel richer. With that in mind, discuss the following questions in your groups.

1 Look at the pictures of the trees opposite and above. What memories from your lifetime do you have of trees? (Have you ever planted one, played in or around one, or cut one down, for example?)

2 List as many types or descriptions of trees as you can.

3 What is your favourite tree? Explain why.

Listen to other people's experiences of trees from around the class. Move around and look at other groups' ideas.

Discuss in your groups the following questions. Spend ten minutes on each and display your ideas around the room.

4 What are the similarities and differences between trees and people?

5 What would it be like if all trees were exactly the same?

6 What have you learned from this discussion about diversity, about yourself, and about others?

Case study 1 – Kew Gardens

Kew Royal Botanical Gardens covers a huge area – 125 hectares – in Richmond, southwest London. They are split into areas including landscaped lawns, formal gardens and greenhouses. It is the largest collection of plants in the world.

The following was written in the visitor book of Kew Gardens by a man who suffers from depression.

'The thought of going to a massive garden in London filled me with dread. I have only ever lived in one house with a garden and all I used it for was to play football and cricket. In fact, we used to play cricket with stones (until either me or my brother hit a six through a neighbour's greenhouse. Sorry.)

Kew Gardens is a fantastic example of how diversity makes our lives richer. There, the gardeners have collected plant species from all over the world. Trees of all different shapes and sizes, and flowers like you have never seen before. The tropical greenhouses contain coffee plants, orchids and lily pads from South America that are bigger than dustbin lids.

When I left Kew Gardens I felt good. Even someone like me, who has never liked flowers or gardening, could not fail to be amazed. When you are amazed by things, it gives you energy. I felt energized and a lot better about life.'

Activities

1 Why do you think the man now feels better about life?

2 Have you ever had a new experience with a place or nature that made you feel better about life? Describe the experience and how it made you feel.

Rules for the global citizen

The Dalai Lama is the leader of the Buddhist community in Tibet, a country that has been invaded by China. He had to flee to India to avoid attack. Even though his country and religion have been destroyed, he is committed to peace and believes it is the only way to change things for the better.

● The Dalai Lama.

Getting technical

Buddhist a member of the religion of Buddhism where people follow the teachings of Buddha.

Activities

1 Which of these 'instructions for life' would you say you live by?

2 Which ones would you like to live by when you get older?

3 Are there any of the 'instructions for life' that you do not agree with? Say why.

Instructions for life in the new millennium from the Dalai Lama

1 Take into account that great love and great achievements involve great risk.

2 When you lose, do not lose the lesson.

3 Follow the 'three Rs': Respect for self, Respect for others, Responsibility for all your actions.

4 Remember that not getting what you want is sometimes a wonderful stroke of luck.

5 Learn the rules so you know how to break them properly.

6 Do not let a little dispute injure a great friendship.

7 When you realize you have made a mistake, take immediate steps to correct it.

8 Spend some time alone every day.

9 Open your arms to change, but do not let go of your values.

10 Remember that silence is sometimes the best answer.

11 Live a good, honourable life. Then, when you get older and think back, you will be able to enjoy it a second time.

12 A loving atmosphere in your home is the foundation for happiness.

13 In disagreements with loved ones, deal only with the current situation.

14 Do not bring up the past.

15 Share your knowledge. It is a way to achieve immortality.

16 Be gentle with the earth.

17 Once a year, go someplace you have never been before.

18 Remember the best relationship is one in which your love for each other exceeds your need for each other.

19 Judge your success by what you had to give up in order to get it.

20 Approach love and cooking with reckless abandon.

Your identities

In order for diversity to be as rich and as interesting as it can, what is the first thing that needs to happen? What do we need to realize about ourselves?

Is anything unique?

Think of all the flowers that you see in gardens, in bunches at the supermarket, and growing wild in the countryside. You can split flowers into groups according to the species. But will all the flowers in these groups be identical? Will they all be the same colour and have the same number of petals, leaves and flower heads? What about the length of the flower stems and the scent each flower gives off? Will they be the same? The more you examine a flower, the more you realize it is unique. At the same time, you can describe groups of flowers, for example, red flowers, or daisies, or flowers with five petals.

Before we can appreciate diversity, we need to appreciate that people are unique individuals who also belong to certain groups and communities. Every single person has a feeling about who they are, what they are like, what they believe and where they belong. This feeling is called identity.

Is one identity enough?

Think about the way you described yourself to your partner. Now think about the way you would describe yourself to:
- someone you are writing to that you had never met before
- someone you might work for
- the coach of a sports team you wanted to join
- a famous actor or popstar.

The ageing process

Think about how you might have described yourself five years ago. Now think about how you might describe yourself in ten years time. Will the descriptions be the same? Why do you think this is?

The main reason that our identities change is that we grow older! As we grow older:
- we experience different things
- we move to different areas
- we gain (and lose) knowledge
- the people around us change
- we begin to value different things.

Activities

In pairs, describe yourself to your partner. Think about:
- your background – where you are from, where you consider your home to be, how you ended up where you are today.
- your likes and dislikes – not just things, but behaviour and feelings as well.
- your interests – what you do and who you do it with.
- your hopes for the future.

When you listen to your partner describe him/herself, listen out for things you did not already know or expect to hear. Jot down any questions you would like to ask your partner. After you have both described yourselves, you can ask your questions. If you ask a question your partner does not want to answer, move on to the next question.

Have a go at writing a description of yourself for someone who does not know you. Your teacher will collect your descriptions and use them for a whole-class activity, so make sure you are happy for everyone to know what you have written.

Changing identities

Group identities

Every single person has their own set of identities. However, we can also experience having a group identity.

Now think about the groups that you belong to. Can you think of any words you could use to describe these groups and communities without describing the individual people that make them up?

Being part of a diverse society is an exciting and interesting experience. Belonging to groups and communities can help us develop our identities and change over time. Can you think of any bad points about having a certain identity or belonging to certain groups or communities? (See activity 3). What is the problem here?

Other people can have false and unfair impressions of us and our groups and communities. When might this have a real impact on our lives? Think about health care, the police, employment and education. Does every individual experience the same treatment and service? How might we change this?

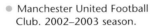

● Manchester United Football Club. 2002–2003 season.

● Members of the public in discussion with police and community representatives.

Activities

1. Make a list of all the groups and communities you belong to. Find three words to describe each group.

2. Make a mindmap of you, your identities, and the groups and communities you belong to.
   a. Put yourself in the centre of the mindmap. Write a short description of yourself.
   b. Now connect out to your different identities. Examples might include 'Year 9 school pupil', 'piano player', 'mosque member', or 'sister'. Write a few words that describe your identity for each one.
   c. Now include all the groups and communities you belong to. Examples might include 'Queen's Heath, Birmingham', 'Middleton School', 'Broxton netball Club', 'family' and 'friends'. Put three words from activity 1 in each group or community.

3. On your mindmap, in a different colour, add words around each entry. These words should describe how other people might see you. For example, as a piano player, other people might see you as clever, artistic and a good person. As one of a group of friends, other people might see you as a bad person. Remember that these words are how other people might see you and are not necessarily what you are really like!

Where in the world did you get that?

- If the words of the English language were a family, what kind of people would they be?
- Would they give new words equal status with the original members of the family?
- Would they soon come to see the newcomers as English words?

Where do you think the following English words were born and how do you think they came to join the family we call the English language? Work in small groups to discuss your ideas. You could use a dictionary with etymology in it to help you. Etymology is the study of the history of words.

- Ketchup
- Hooligan
- Penguin
- Sauna
- Mammoth

- Robot
- Coffee
- Cheetah
- Marmalade
- Hurricane

- Budgerigar
- Satsuma
- Bizarre
- Caravan
- Ski

- Paprika
- Tea
- Tattoo
- Ukulele
- Chimpanzee

Ketchup was introduced in Victorian times.

Toy robots became popular in the 1950s

Penguin species are found on every continent in the Southern Hemisphere

Use a map of the world to find the original homes for the words in the list on the opposite page.

Wales	Spain (near French border –	Hawaii
Ireland	Basque territory)	Africa
Norway	Turkey	Polynesian islands
Finland	India	Caribbean islands
Russia	Iran	Australia
The Czech Republic	China	Malaysia
Hungary	Japan	France

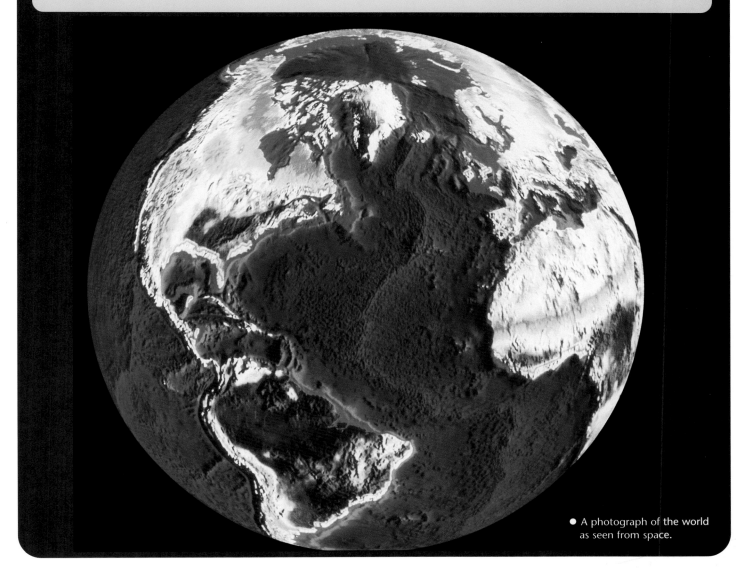

● A photograph of the world as seen from space.

English has freely adopted words from many other languages. Our language has changed and grown over time and has become enriched by the additions. Both the words and what they represent have become part of our lives and have helped us learn about the world. Can you think of any other words in the English language that have come from other countries? Write a list of as many as you can think of. In your list, try to include the country that each word came from.

Cultural diversity – what is on the menu?

The history of Britain has had an important part to play in enriching our culture – and our food! The Romans brought us cherries, peas and cabbages and, strange as it may seem, stinging nettles for use as vegetables.

The Saxons had a flair for growing herbs; the Vikings brought expertise in drying and smoking fish, and the Normans encouraged us to drink wine. In the twelfth century, the Crusaders were the first to try oranges and lemons. Later, in the Tudor period, we used spices from the Far East and potatoes, which originally came from America.

What some people thought of as traditional British food in the mid-twentieth century has changed too. British cuisine used to be thought of as roast beef, steak and kidney pie, and the favourite take-away was fish and chips.

Getting technical

Crusader a knight who fought in the Holy Land (near Jerusalem) to regain Christian holy places from the Saracens in the eleventh century.

● Today T.V. chefs use ingredients from all over the world.

Food for thought

The more diverse our society becomes, the more choice and variety we have in our supermarkets and on our plates. This makes our diet richer and more enjoyable.

Getting technical

Cuisine fine foods.

Activities

1 As a whole class, plan a tasting challenge where each member of the group brings in a snack from around the world.

2 Devise a questionnaire that asks about appeal to the eye and to the taste buds.

3 Present your finding as a bar or 'pie' chart and display and produce a map representing the groups' favourite tasty treats.

By 1950, tastes were beginning to change. A food writer called Elizabeth David startled her readers by bringing out *A Book of Mediterranean Food*. Today, we can sample cuisine from all around the world, and what was considered typically British has changed as Britain has changed and evolved. Think about the food you eat.

Activities

4 How many different types of cuisine are offered in the restaurants in your area?

5 List some dishes you might associate with 'take-aways'.

6 Why do you think British tastes have changed in the last few decades?

7 Is there a particular dish that is associated with your town, city or country?

Extension Activity

8 Ask a relative or neighbour who is over 50 how the food that is available and popular today is different from what he/she remembers from his/her childhood. Write down what he/she says.

9 Look at the range of food offered in your school canteen. How many different countries of origin can you trace the dishes back to?

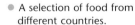
● A selection of food from different countries.

In common

All things are bound together.
All things connect.
What happens to the Earth
Happens to the children of the Earth.
Man has not woven the web of life.
He's but one thread.
Whatever he does to the web
He does to himself.

Chief Seattle, 1865

Activities

1. Read the poem *In Common*. What is meant by the words, 'All things are bound together. All things connect'?

2. In what ways are the people in your class connected?

3. How is your class connected to the rest of the school, to other young people in the community, to everyone in Britain, to the world?

4. Think of a time when you felt isolated and compare it to a time when you felt connected. Describe the differences in your feelings to someone in the class. You can describe yourself in the two different situations through writing – such as a poem or a story – or producing a drawing that represents the different emotions you felt.

Extension Activity

5. In groups, research and script a series of items for a television show for teenagers on the theme of 'Connection with others'.

   Present your show to the rest of the class.

● Human beings are sociable and like the company of others.

Teaching others about the value of diversity

There are 6 billion people living on the earth. Every single person is connected to other people in different ways. These connections can be through families, jobs, hobbies, interests, likes, dislikes, health, education, feelings, and so on. Think how many connections exist between all the people in the world.

The best way to learn something is to teach it. Work as a group to create an activity for younger pupils to show how everyone is connected. Below is an example of a game called 'Web of Life' that demonstrates how interconnected we all are.

You will need a large ball of string or wool to play the game.

Activities

1. After you have looked at this game you can play it and try to adapt it. The aim will be to teach younger pupils about being 'connected'. Or you can develop another game or a script outline for a film, which involves a whole group of people realizing that they had more in common than they think.

2. What films or stories have you enjoyed that help connect you to others who are different from you?

   What particular scenes can you remember?

Rules

All students and the teacher need to sit or stand in a circle. One person can hold the ball of wool or string in their hand and say: 'My name is _____ and I like (an activity). Who else likes _____?' They then pass the ball of string to whoever replies. This person then repeats the sentence but chooses a different thing to say about him/herself. For example, I might say, 'My name is Joe and I like playing football. Who else likes playing football?' As the game goes on, the students will become connected by a web of wool/string. Building this web can help people to learn how they are interconnected because when someone tugs on one part of the web, other people in the web are affected.

Some films and stories give very powerful messages about being 'connected'. Connections are the most important things in life. This is why so many films and books are written with 'connections' as the theme. The story might be about falling in love, finding someone who was lost, rebuilding a relationship, making friends with enemies, discovering new experiences with people, or simply someone being true to their own feelings and discovering things about themselves.

HUGH GRANT   ANDIE MACDOWELL

A MIKE NEWELL FILM

● Romantic comedy: Four Weddings and a Funeral

Case study 2 – Diversity and inspiration

V.S. Naipaul is an author who was awarded the Nobel Prize for Literature 2001 for his work.

Naipaul was born in Trinidad in 1932 and has lived in Britain since 1950. His parents were Hindu immigrants from Northern India. He was inspired by his father who was a journalist and who told him not to be frightened to be an artist. He says of himself: 'I wanted to be famous. I also wanted to be a writer; to be famous for writing. And the strange thing was that I had no idea what I was going to write about.'

He did, however, find much to write about and has written over twenty-five works including articles, essays and novels. In them, he blends the worlds of British street life and remembers India, as well as many other locations around the world. He says of his time of inspiration: 'One day, deep in my depression, I began to see what my material might be: the city street that I stood back from and the country life before that, with the ways and manners of a remembered India.'

● V.S. Naipaul accepts the Nobel Prize.

Getting technical

Nobel Prize prize awarded for achievement in physics, chemistry, medicine, literature and peace. Named after the Swedish chemist Alfred Nobel who left a fortune as a foundation for the Nobel prizes,

Activities

V.S. Naipaul uses his experience of different cultures and traditions to write his books. He also talks of being inspired by his father.

1. Imagine you are looking back on your life and thinking about what influenced and inspired you. What would you pick out from your experiences now that might stay with you in the future?

2. What do you think that life on earth would have been like if no one travelled and ideas, languages, food and nature never experienced diversity?

Extension Activity

The Booker Prize for Literature was established in 1968 and rewards the best novel of the year by a citizen of the Commonwealth or Northern Ireland. Winners usually reflect a wide variety of cultural backgrounds.

3. Find out (perhaps on the Internet) which novels have won the Booker Prize for Literature over the last 20 years.

4. Summarise the themes explored in each book and explain when and where the story is set.

5. Present your findings in a booklet for the school library. Call it '20 years of the Booker winners'. Aim to show the variety of cultural and historical experiences in the novels. Think about ways to make the booklet eye-catching as well as informative.

Refugees, asylum seekers and diversity

Some people are a bit unsure as to what refugees and asylum seekers are. A 'refugee' is a person who has fled from his or her home or is unable to return to it. This is because they are afraid of being persecuted for reasons of race, religion, nationality or membership of a particular social group or political opinion. An 'asylum seeker' is a person who has had to leave their country because they would be in danger if they stayed. They are looking for shelter in a country where they will be safe.

As you will see from some of the case studies in this chapter, many influencial men and women in history who were once asylum seekers have made a positive difference to the world. These people became more creative and determined because they had some experience of living in different cultures.

Think of some of your experiences with people from other cultures and how these experiences have helped you to see things in a different way.

● Refugees in make-shift homes.

Getting technical

Refugees are people who have had to leave a country and are unable to return to their home. This is because they are afraid of being persecuted for reasons of race, religion, nationality, membership of a particular group or political opinion.

Asylum seekers are people who have had to leave their country because they would be in danger if they stayed. They are looking for shelter in a country where they would be safe.

Political opinion the views people have about who they might vote for or what other causes they are prepared to support or protest against.

Activities

1. List the reasons why people move from one country to another.

2. Has anyone in your family's history had to flee their home? If so, where did they go and why?

3. Work in a group to answer the following questions. State whether the following statements are true or false. You may need to do some research to help you decide.

   - 80% of the world's refugee population lives outside Europe.
   - Britain is the most popular destination for asylum seekers in Europe.
   - Most refugees are women and children.
   - Refugees have never made positive contributions to the country they now inhabit.
   - Asylum seekers in the UK are not allowed to work at all for six months.
   - Many asylum seekers are in the UK illegally.
   - Asylum seekers are not allowed to claim social security benefits.
   - In 2002, a single adult asylum seeker was entitled to claim only £37.77 a week from the government.
   - In 2001, the United Nations High Commissioner for Refugees criticized the British media for provoking racial hatred.
   - In 2002, a report published by the Association of Chief Police Officers said that there was no evidence for a higher rate of crime among refugees and asylum seekers in the UK.

Case study 3 – pride in a new country

Mohammed was arrested and tortured by Iraqi police as a teenager. Eventually he escaped with his father and studied at Oxford University and the Royal College of Surgeons in Dublin. He became an Irish citizen in 1990 and has lectured in medicine, worked as a doctor in Dublin hospitals, and written and lectured widely on human rights and the care of survivors of torture.

'I am proud to be Irish and I feel I have contributed to the health of this nation. I also believe I have added "colour" to Ireland in more ways than one,' he says with a smile.

Fame academy of refugees

The following individuals were refugees in different countries.

Jesus Christ – his family fled with him as a baby from Israel to Egypt.

Albert Einstein (1879–1955) – a Jewish physicist who fled from Nazi Germany to the UK and then to the USA.

Thomas Mann (1875–1955) – winner of the Nobel prize for literature in 1929. He fled Nazi Germany to Switzerland and eventually lived in the USA.

Ovid (43BC–17AD) – Roman poet who was exiled by the emperor Augustus. His writing heavily influenced Shakespeare.

Frederic Chopin (1810–49) – after he left his native Poland to pursue a musical career, his country was invaded by Russia. He was not allowed to return and spent his life in Paris where he composed many great pieces of classical music.

Victor Hugo (1802–85) – French writer who was forced to leave his native land in 1851. His novels included *Les Miserables* and *The Hunchback of Notre Dame*.

Madeleine Korbel Albright (b. 1937) – the first woman ever to hold the position of Secretary of State in the USA. She was twice a refugee, whose family fled from Nazi Germany and then later from Czechoslovakia.

Sitting Bull (1830–90) – Tatanka Iyotake (Sitting Bull) was one of the most famous Indian tribal leaders. His Sioux nation was invaded by the US army despite a protected treaty between the Sioux people and the US government. He and the remaining part of his people eventually fled to Canada where he was killed by white soldiers.

Activities

1. Find out more about these refugees and present your research in the form of a display.

2. Research on the Internet, other famous refugees who have had a positive influence in the country where they have settled.

Review and reflect

What is diversity?

This unit has examined the nature of diversity.
Perhaps diversity can be thought of in this way:

Different
Individuals
Valuing
Each other
Regardless of
Skin,
Intellect,
Talents, or
Years.

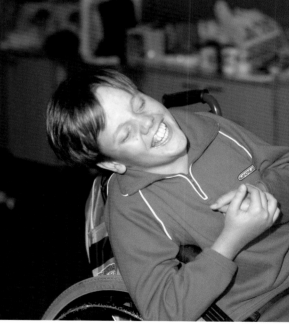

Activities

If there was no diversity what would the world be like?

Chapter 3

Global issues

Learn about...

- How events in one country affect us all.
- How the future of the environment impacts on everyone.
- How individuals and groups can make a difference.

Every day you see and hear the phrases global warming, climate change, greenhouse effect, drought, poverty, famine, globalization, multinationals, fair trade, ethical trade, the global village. All these phrases remind us that we live in an interdependent world. We also live on a planet where the plants, the animals and the natural resources need to find a balance. Human activities threaten that balance.

People of all ages are joining pressure groups like Greenpeace and the WWF (World Wildlife Fund for Nature). Many people want to make a difference and feel that by taking part and protesting they can make a difference. Do you agree?

With fast travel, the Internet, satellites and television, our world is becoming more and more interlinked. Businesses, cultures, countries and people all fit into one huge jigsaw puzzle. No one country can survive alone. Is this a good thing or a bad thing?

Getting technical

Global issues that affect the whole planet.
Pressure groups groups who campaign to bring about change by influencing governments and companies.
Fair trading a trading system that makes sure the people who grow or make the product get a fair price for their work.
Ethical trading a trading system where companies have agreed certain rules about their trading practices, and how they treat their workers, to make sure that the environment is protected and their workers are respected.

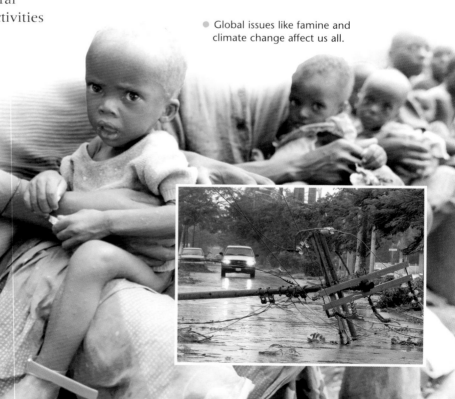

- Global issues like famine and climate change affect us all.

How interdependent are you?

The picture shows a typical teenage boy and girl and their likely possessions. We all know the importance of fashion and wearing the right 'label', but where are these goods made?

Look at your possessions. How many were made in the UK? How many were made in the European Union (EU)? How many come from less economically developed countries (LEDCs)? How many were made in the Far East or China? Make a list of all the countries your possessions come from. Why do you think they were made there? Often the answer has to do with money. But is this the only important thing?

- Your trainers may have been made by poorly paid people, even young children.
- Your fast food may have come from cattle raised on land that used to be lush rainforest.
- The factory that made your CD player may be polluting a nearby river.

Campaigners and protesters are becoming very concerned about the world's natural resources and the way people (individuals, companies and countries) trade.

Activities

① Why is it cheaper for companies to make goods abroad and transport them to the UK instead of making them in the UK?

② Events like Live Aid and Comic Relief raise millions of pounds for charities. How do you think they should spend their money?

③ Using the Internet or other resources, investigate the work of one national or international environmental pressure group.

Extension Activity

④ Plan an event for your own school to raise money for an international group.
- What cause would you choose and why?
- What event(s) would you organize?
- How would you work with others to organize these events?
- How would you promote your event?

Getting technical

Interdependent a term used to explain how people, companies and countries can no longer work alone, but have to rely on others.

European Union a group of European contries, currently 15 including the United Kingdom. They work together to improve their trade. The EU passes laws which affect all member countries. In 2004, ten more countries will be joining.

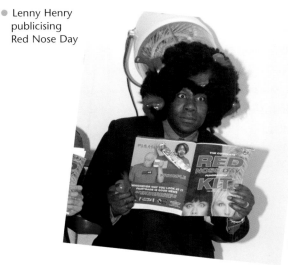

● Lenny Henry publicising Red Nose Day

The Amazon

We are going to study the impact of 'deforestation' (cutting down the forest) in the Amazon rainforest in Brazil. Do you know where Brazil is? Perhaps it is too far away to be a concern. But the impact of this deforestation is having an effect upon us all.

What do we know about Brazil?

Brazil is the largest country in South America. It is the fifth largest country in the world after Russia, China, Canada and the US.

Sao Paulo in Brazil is the third largest city in the world, with over 20 million people. The total population of Brazil in 2003 was 179 million. Fourteen of its cities have populations of over 1 million people and 80 per cent of its population live in cities.

Over 66 per cent of Brazil's land surface is covered in forest.

What impression do the facts give you about Brazil? How does it compare with the UK?

● The burning of the Amazon rainforest viewed from space

Fact sheet

The Amazon rainforest contains:

- 1 in 6 of all the world's birds
- 1 in 11 of all the world's mammals
- 1 in 15 of all the world's reptiles
- 20 per cent of the earth's fresh water

Getting technical

Deforestation cutting down trees for timber and to make way for farming and industry.

Rainforest dense, evergreen forest, which grows around the equator in a very hot and wet climate.

● Brazil and the Amazon rainforest

Rainforest in Brazil

Rainforest in South America

0   662   1324km

1cm on the map = 662km on the ground

Why is the Amazon rainforest important?

The rainforest covers 5.5 million square kilometres. This area is equal to about half the size of Europe. Since 1970, over ten per cent of the forest has been destroyed – an area the size of France.

A typical hectare of rainforest has 250 different types of tree, compared with ten per hectare in Europe. The huge trees in this hot and humid environment form a canopy where little light gets in. This canopy has a huge population of birds, including macaws and toucans, and a vast number of mammals, including bats. The rivers running through the forest contain over 1500 different fish species. The forest is a rich and diverse ecosystem.

Over 10 million people live in the rainforest. They rely on the natural resources of the forest to survive.

So is it important to protect the Amazon rainforest? What do you think?

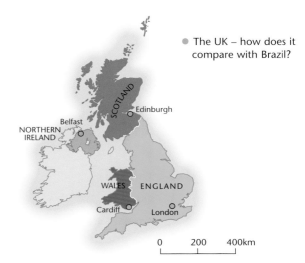

● The UK – how does it compare with Brazil?

0   200   400km

1cm on the map = 200km on the ground

Getting technical

Ecosystem where different species live alongside each other and maintain a balanced natural environment.
Hectare 100 x 100 metres

Activities

1. Draw up a table to compare Brazil and the UK. Use the following headings: Size, Population, Number of cities over 1 million population. Do some research and find out how our wealth and raw materials differs from that of Brazil.

2. Why should we be worried about deforestation?

3. Design a poster to draw attention to the wildlife under threat due to deforestation.

Extension Activity

4. Research and prepare a report called 'Background on Brazil'. The report could be used later to provide 'expert' evidence in a class debate about deforestation.

● The lush and dense undergrowth of the Amazon rainforest.

Why is the world concerned?

Every year about one per cent of the Amazon rainforest is disappearing. If this rate carries on, the forest might totally disappear in your lifetime.

What's the problem?

So what is it all about? How does it affect us? We have already seen that plants and animals are losing their homes. But there is another serious problem. Much of the land is cleared by burning. Huge fires give off dense smoke, which blocks the sun's light over vast areas. Many local people develop lung diseases.

The rainforest plays a major part in the climate of the whole world. The trees and vegetation take in carbon dioxide. This is the gas that causes global warming. So rainforests help to stop global warming. The plants also give out oxygen, which we all need to breathe and live. This means that deforestation may have a huge impact over the whole world, leading to more global warming and less oxygen. This is how it affects us. This is the greenhouse effect.

Fact sheet

Global rainforest destruction

Global destruction rate

1 second	=	1 hectare
1 minute	=	60 hectares
1 day	=	86,000 hectares
1 year	=	31 million hectares (larger than the size of the UK)

● Burning and clearing the rainforest.

There is another serious global issue about deforestation. There are so many species of plants and animals that some have not even been discovered yet! What if we lose these species before we even know they exist? Why would this be a problem? Think about this – many medicines for illness and diseases come from plants and animals found in the rainforest. Think how many more medicines we might find there. But only if we stop destroying the rainforest.

Cutting down trees leads to 35 species becoming extinct every day. Is this acceptable?

● Wildlife under threat from deforestation in the Amazon rainforest.

Getting technical

Greenhouse effect changes in the world's climate because of increased carbon dioxide in the atmosphere. This is resulting in rising temperatures around the world.

Activities

1 How does the rainforest affect the climate of the world?

2 Write a letter to a newspaper outlining the reasons why the whole world should be concerned about the destruction of the Amazon rainforest.

Extension Activity

3 Working with others, design a poster, using the figures from this section and ones you have researched, to get the message across that something must be done about deforestation.

Why is deforestation taking place?

In Brazil, most people live in large crowded cities. The indigenous people who live in the rainforest understand how to live in harmony with the rainforest. But other people began to move in and the forest has become endangered.

Roads

Brazil has a huge highway that runs through the Amazon rainforest. Thousands of trees were felled to make way for it.

Logging

The new roads made it easier for logging companies to get into the forest. Sometimes huge areas are cleared just to find a few valuable trees like the Brazilian mahogany. The trees are cut down, sawn up and shipped all over the world.

● A Brazilian cattle ranch.

Settlement

After the roads were built, some Brazilians moved from towns and cities into the rainforest. They cleared land for farming crops like maize, sugar and coffee. Again, the soil soon becomes infertile so more land is cleared. Many people have given up and moved back to the towns and cities.

RORAIMA
AMAPÁ
Belém
Manaus
AMAZONAS
PARÁ
MARANHÃO
Fortaleza
Natal
ACRE
B R A Z I L
Recife
RONDÔNIA
MATO GROSSO
BAHIA
Salvador
GOIÁS
Brasília

Rainforest

MINAS GERAIS
Belo Horizonte

Atlantic Ocean

Rio de Janeiro
São Paulo
Curtiba

0   500   1000km

Porto Alegre

Cattle ranching

This is to blame for 80 per cent of the deforestation. The government sold land very cheaply to large companies for clearing and raising cattle for beef. For the first few years the soil allowed the pasture to grow. But after a few years, the soil had become too poor and more land needed to be cleared.

Gold rush

In the 1980s, several large gold discoveries were made in the rainforest and miners moved in. This 'gold rush' had a large impact on the forest. Land had to be cleared for airfields, towns, mining camps and quarries. Mercury was used to extract gold and this polluted the rivers.

Mineral extraction

The Amazon rainforest contains a vast wealth of minerals other than gold: tin, silver, manganese, iron ore and bauxite. A development at Carajás mines the largest iron ore deposits in the world. The trees are cleared to make way for the quarries, the processing factories, and to provide fuel for smelting the iron ore.

Hydro-electric dams

Since the 1960s the government has built several hydro-electric dams. This has led to the destruction of thousands of hectares of rainforest and the flooding of some Indian Reserves.

Fifty years ago, the government of Brazil was faced with the problems of:

- a rapidly rising population
- a lack of land for farming and building
- massive cities unable to expand.

What should it have done? Where did it go wrong?

Getting technical

Indigenous people groups of people who have traditionally lived in an area.
World Bank this was established in 1947 to promote economic development by lending to Less Economically Developed Countries (LEDCs).

● A hydro-electric dam.

Activities

1. Write a newspaper article, dated 1955, explaining the benefits of moving out of the cities to the rainforest.

2. What positive impact might the developments in the rainforests have had?

3. What changes would you have made to the schemes that the government encouraged?

4. Some of the money for these developments came from the World Bank. Pressure groups now encourage the Bank to attach conditions to any future loans it makes. What do you think are the three most important conditions they should attach to any new loans?

Extension Activity

5. In a group, divide into two teams.

   Team A are to design a poster showing the benefits that the developments above have brought to Brazil.
   Team B are to design a poster showing the problems associated with these developments.

A case study – Acre

Acre is in western Brazil. It borders Peru and Bolivia. Its population in 1996 was 483,600, of whom 201,300 lived in Rio Branco, its capital.

Life in Acre is dominated by the Amazon rainforest. Ninety-three per cent of the 55,000 square miles of Acre is tropical rainforest.

In recent years Acre has seen many changes. Wealthy ranchers, poor farmers, city merchants, workers, miners, loggers and rubber tappers have all moved in to compete for natural resources. These groups have often come into conflict with the Native Indians.

The indigenous Indians of Acre belong mainly to two groups: the Pano and Aruaque. They live by hunting, fishing and farming, and live mainly by the riverside inside the forest. But the population growth has meant that their way of life is under threat. As land is cleared, the Native Indians are forced off the land and become homeless. Sometimes they move to the poor districts of the cities. But they have no money and are usually unable to read or write.

0   662   1324km

1cm on the map = 662km on the ground

ACRE

BRAZIL

BR364

Sena Madureira

A C R E

Rio Branco

0   250km

● Forced to live off what others throw away.

● Native Indian of Acre.

The BR364 highway

The BR364 connects Acre with the rest of Brazil. The highway means that the cattle ranchers, loggers and mining companies can move people in and raw materials out. The government plans to continue the road through Acre to connect Brazil with Peru and the Pacific coast. The impact of this on the rainforest will be immense.

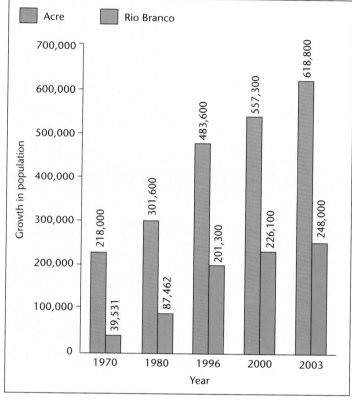

● Population growth in Acre and Rio Branco 1970–2003.

Making a difference

On 22 December 1988, Chico Mendes was murdered in Xapun, Acre. He was a rubber tapper and an environmental activist. He was keen for land to be made into reserves for native people. In 1987 the United Nations Organization awarded him a 'Global 500 Award'.

In 1990, two landowners were found guilty of his murder and sentenced to nineteen years in prison. In 1993 they escaped but were captured again in 1996.

The murder of Chico Mendes and the organization set up after his death have helped to draw attention to the problems of the Native Indians who are murdered, threatened and deprived of their land and rights.

Getting technical

Environmental activist individuals who are concerned about the environment and campaign on environmental issues.
Global 500 Awards established in 1967 by the United Nations Environment Programme, these are annual awards to individuals and organisations who have made outstanding contribution towards protecting and improving the environment.

Activities

1. How has Acre changed since 1970?

2. Draw up a list indicating the positive and negative changes that have taken place in Acre since 1970.

3. Does the extension of BR364 to the Pacific pose a threat or opportunity? Give reasons for your answer.

Extension Activity

4. Not many people know about Acre. Following some research, design a leaflet for people visiting Acre, outlining what Acre and its people are like. Compare your leaflet with others in your class. How are they similar? How are they different? Now you have seen other leaflets, is there anything you would change about yours?

Are there any sustainable solutions?

What should or can be done?

It is crucial that we stop deforestation. Doing nothing will not help. Time is running out.

But is it enough just to stop the activities that destroy the forest? Remember that millions of people live in, or near, rainforests. Many of them live in poverty. How can we develop sustainable rainforests? This means developing them so that they are not destroyed and so that people can improve their lives.

Many organizations and pressure groups have become involved in protecting the rainforests, while allowing sustainable development. The Brazilian government is now involved in bringing about change. It has worked with other groups to make sure that over the next ten years at least ten per cent of the rainforest will be set aside and protected.

Other groups have applied pressure to the World Bank and industrial countries to use their power to protect the forests.

Some groups help Native Indians fight legal cases to protect their land. The Indians are now working with environmentalists to find a sustainable way of farming without destroying the forest. Now 31 per cent of the forest has been reserved for the Native Indian population.

The first large sustainable development is in Mamirana. The 20,000 Native Indians living in villages there are being encouraged to stay and play a major part in protecting the natural resources. Harvests have increased and a new source of earnings from 'eco-tourism' is growing larger each year. As the local population has benefited, they have taken on the responsibility for policing conservation laws in their local area.

Does it make economic sense?

Options:
- If one hectare is used as cattle pasture, it raises $148.
- If it is cut for timber, it raises $1000.
- If the forest is protected and sustainably farmed for fruits, latex and timber, it raises $6820.

In 1988, the Brazilian government created the first sustainable logging project on land owned by Native Indians in the rainforest. The project is partly funded by the World Bank and will allow the Xikrim tribe to sell mahogany and other woods directly to buyers across the world. The government hopes this will stop large logging companies from destroying the forest in tribal reservations.

● Rubbertapping in the rainforest.

In Acre, the governor Jorge Viana is aiming to make 25 per cent of Acre rainforest part of a sustainable forest management scheme. A total of 4 million hectares would be safeguarded. The WWF has rewarded Governor Viana with the 'Gift of the Earth Award'. To prove his commitment, Governor Viana has ordered that any timber bought in Acre must come from sustainable developments that have been properly managed.

Is tourism the answer?

Even with all these changes, the Amazon is so vast that it is almost impossible to control illegal deforestation.

The government of Brazil is now trying a different approach – eco-tourism. It is spending large sums of money to develop tourism based on the natural environment.

According to the Brazilian government, 'People can make money from the rainforest without destroying it. It is just a matter of showing them how.'

The rainforest is attracting tourism from all over the world. One visitor said: 'It is all so pure, so absolutely unspoiled and I think it is awesome.' One of the attractions of the rainforest is the scale of its biodiversity – there are so many different plants and animals.

Tourists hire local guides to learn about the forest and travel by river, where they visit remote villages and buy crafts made by the villagers. They stay at hostels and hotels built into the jungle. The eco-tourism boom has created lots of new jobs and put money into the Native Indian economy.

● Eco-tourists visiting the rainforest.

● Native Indians selling traditional hand-made goods.

Activities

1. Using examples, how would you explain the term 'sustainability'?

2. What are the advantages of 'eco-tourism' to Brazil?

3. How do you think the Native Indians feel about eco-tourism?

4. Design a poster for an eco-tourist holiday in the Amazon rainforest.

Extension Activity

5. Investigate some real brochures on eco-tourist holidays in the Amazon rainforest.

6. Design your own brochure, including a ten-day timetable. Use the Internet and ICT to help you.

Getting technical

Sustainable activities that use the environment without destroying it.

Biodiversity a wide range of plants and animals living together in the same area.

Eco-tourism encouraging tourists to visit an area because of its environmental importance. This form of 'low impact' tourism is supposed to be friendly to the environment.

Reflect and review

This chapter of the book has dealt with issues thousands of miles away from the UK but issues that impact on our lives today and in the future.

What are the key issues?

- Care of the environment.
- How to deal with a growing population.
- How do we encourage economic development in less economically developed countries?
- Do indigenous people have 'rights'?
- Should we be concerned about climate change?
- Should organizations like the World Bank make conditions when they lend money?
- Do pressure groups make a difference?
- Can we as individuals make a difference?

All these important issues are involved in your consideration of the deforestation of the Amazon rainforest.

How and why did things go wrong?

Who do you blame? The decision of the Brazilians 40 years ago?

Faced with their population and economic needs, what would you have done?

If the issues that are involved in the Amazon rainforest affect the whole world, who should make the decisions that bring about change?

● Pressure groups across the world protest about the destruction of the rainforests.

The Amazon debate

Now that you have completed this chapter, you need to review what you have learned. Do this in a group. To make this more interesting, look back over the chapter, imagining you are either:

- Native Indians, or
- members of the Brazilian government, or
- environmentalists, or
- poor people in one of Brazil's huge cities.

Write a summary report of your group's viewpoint. Include your thoughts on questions like:

- Should the rainforest be used for any development?
- Was the government wrong to allow all development?
- Should Brazilian people be forced to live in cities to stop them moving into the rainforest?
- Should tourists be allowed into the rainforest?
- Should Native Indians not have any new buildings, electricity, cars and modern household items?
- Should the rest of the world have a say in the future of the rainforest?

Write down any other thoughts or feelings you have.

You can use the Internet or library resources to find out more. You could also use travel brochures and leaflets about the rainforest.

Now imagine you have to present your viewpoint in a debate. What will you include? What will you leave out? If you have only ten minutes for your group to speak, who will say what? Will you illustrate your talk?

● Farmers selling their products.

● Living conditions for the poor.

● Heavy industry in the rainforest.

Chapter 4

What is conflict?

This chapter will explore the ideas of 'conflict' and 'peace'. It will consider some religious views about them. We will ask questions like: What is conflict? Is it always a bad thing? If nobody likes to suffer, why do conflicts happen? Is there any way of ridding the world of conflict?

Learn about...

- Different types and levels of conflict.
- Different causes of conflict.
- Conflict resolution.
- Religious attitudes towards conflict and conflict resolution.

Activities

1 Use the 'Brainstorm food' box below to see if you can identify different types of conflict. For example, 'tug-of-war' might make you think of 'friendly conflict' or 'agreed conflict'.

> **Brainstorm food**
> Boxing   9/11   Bullying
> Tug-of-war   Environmental protesters
>   Atomic War   Confusion
> Jerusalem   Family arguments
> Anne Frank   Politicians   Dilemma
>   Martin Luther King   Northern Ireland

2 Think about whether there are different *levels* of conflict.
 a Are physical conflicts on the same level as verbal conflicts in your view?
 b Does the level of conflict differ if just two people are involved, or 1000?
 Add any ideas you have about how each type of conflict might have different levels.

It is easy to think of 'conflicts' as 'wars' that we see reported on the TV news. But there are many different *types* of conflict such as those between two people, two sports teams, or two religions, as well as two countries.

- Is boxing a type of 'conflict'? Why or why not?

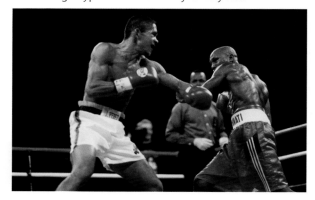

3 Try to come up with your own examples of conflict (perhaps one or two for each type of conflict you identified). Are there any other types of conflict you could add now? Write these down.

4 Is there anything that all conflicts have in common? With a neighbour, try to define what you think a 'conflict' is. Perhaps write a sentence starting 'All conflicts are...' See what others think too!

5 Is it possible to have a conflict with yourself? How does it feel and how does it make you think? Reflect for a moment or two and give some examples to explain your views.

6 Choose one of the quotes in the Quote Box and discuss it in a group. Is conflict always bad? When, if ever, is conflict useful or good?

● The Battle of the Somme 1916. On the first day alone, 50,000 allied soldiers were slaughtered in terrible conditions. What type and level of conflict would you call this?

Getting technical

Conflict a struggle, fight or disagreement.
Contraries opposites e.g. love and hate.

Quote box

'An eye for an eye makes the whole world blind.'
Gandhi

'Without contraries there is no progression. Attraction and repulsion, reason and energy, love and hate, are necessary to human existence.'
The Marriage of Heaven and Hell, William Blake

'No, when the fight begins within himself,
A man's worth something.'
Bishop Blougram's Apology, Robert Browning

Media challenge

In small groups, and using only one newspaper, how many stories or examples of conflict can you find? Cut out the headlines and list them under these three types of conflict:

- personal conflict (conflict between two people)
- community conflict (conflict between two communities within a country)
- international conflict (conflict between two countries).

Activities

1 Could some examples be put into more than one type of conflict? If so, why?

2 From your newspaper, which is the most common type of conflict?

3 Do you think this is the most common type of conflict in the world? Or do you think newspapers have ignored other types of conflicts? Why might they do that?

4 Are there any clues in the articles as to why the conflict was happening? What were the causes of conflict in the examples you discovered?

5 See if you can find one conflict reported by two different papers. Have they got the same facts and views about it? If they are different, how do you know which one to believe?

Why do conflicts happen?

If all human beings want to be happy, why do we allow conflicts to happen at all? They can create so much suffering. This section will help you to investigate the causes of conflict – why conflicts happen in the world around us. This is important because understanding how conflicts are caused may help us to avoid them in the future or give us some ideas as to how we might resolve conflicts once they have started.

You have seen how there can be many types and levels of conflict. The First World War is different in many ways, for example, to an argument between two parents or neighbours. But do these examples have common causes, even though they are of different types and levels? How can we tell? Perhaps we need to break these complicated areas down into more simple parts so that we can understand them more easily.

Activities

1 Think of a particular conflict, one that you know something about. It might be a conflict in school, at home, from history, the news, or a 'soap' on TV. Briefly describe the conflict.

2 Now, using the conflict chart on the right, break down the conflict situation into more simple parts. Each section represents the views of one person or group involved in the conflict. This will help you to understand the situation more clearly.

Who? Name one group or person involved in the conflict. There may be just two altogether, or many more.

Needs or desires? Write down what that group or person needs or wants in this situation. It might be an object, a feeling, a result of some sort, or perhaps a combination of all of these.

Fears? What does that group or person fear or not want in this situation?

Common ground? What does that group or person have in common with the others involved in the conflict? For example, do they like the same things, come from a similar place, or share the same needs or fears?

Who? Needs? Fears? Common ground? — Who? Needs? Fears? Common ground? — CONFLICT — Who? Needs? Fears? Common ground? — Who? Needs? Fears? Common ground?

Cartoon by Peter Brookes in *The Times*, 15 February 2001

● What does this cartoon suggest to you about conflict and its causes?

3 Do you think that each person or group involved knows what the others need or fear? Are they aware of any common ground between them? Put a tick beside those who know and a cross beside those who do not know.

4 Now study the conflict chart carefully. With a partner, discuss what you think the causes of the conflict are in this situation. Write a few sentences below the chart to explain your views. (Use the Ideas Box below to help you, but do think of your own too!)

5 Look at the 'common ground' parts of the chart. What ideas might these give you about how the conflict might be resolved?

Extension Activity

6 Think back to the examples of conflict in the introduction to this unit. Do you think that an argument between neighbours or parents and the First World War have common causes behind the conflicts? Has doing the conflict chart helped you to answer this question? If so, how?

Ideas box

'There isn't enough for everybody.' 'They didn't feel safe.' 'They needed more.' 'Revenge!' 'Proving something to others.' 'Enough is enough.' 'They just wouldn't listen.' 'Old scores being settled.' 'Fear on both sides.' 'Greed.' 'Ignorance of others' views.' 'Desperation.' 'Desire for freedom.' 'Wouldn't back down.'

Can conflicts be justified?

When, if ever, would you be prepared to fight in a war? When, in your opinion, would there be good reason to fire bullets at other human beings or drop bombs on living targets from a fighter plane? Is it ever right to kill other human beings? This section will look at Christian attitudes towards conflict and war in particular. Will you agree or disagree with these Christian views?

● When, if ever, would you be willing to release bombs on human targets?

● Would you have refused to fight in the Second World War?

Christian attitudes towards war

Pacifist Christians

Jesus taught on many occasions that loving others (especially your enemies), forgiving wrongdoers, and making peace in the world, are important ways to know God more closely and live a good life. For this reason, many Christians are 'pacifists' – people who believe in strictly non-violent solutions to the world's problems. To harm or kill others is to destroy what God has created and to ignore the teachings of Jesus. Violence, they argue, will only create more violence.

But not all Christians are pacifists. While all of them would agree with 'loving your neighbour', some Christians might also believe that war is, at times, a 'necessary evil'. Trying to stop Adolf Hitler in 1939 by 'loving him', for example, would not work. He would not listen to others and would continue to rule over Europe and kill millions of people in the process. Fighting his army was tragic, painful and 'unloving', but also necessary to avoid a much worse situation.

Getting technical

Pacifist a 'peace person'; one who believes in non-violence.

Christians and just war

Some Christians therefore believe that war is necessary, but five very important conditions need to be met first. If they are, the war is seen as 'just' or morally acceptable, and those Christians may then agree to fight in it.

The five conditions of a just war

1 The war must be declared by a legal and recognised authority (a government, for example).

2 The cause of the war must be 'just'. The intention of going to war must be for good moral reasons or to prevent evil.

3 The war must be the last resort. All other methods of trying to prevent armed conflict must have been attempted.

4 The war must be fought with enough force to achieve the goals, but no more; the force used must be 'in proportion'.

5 The war must not – as far as possible – involve innocent people or destroy civilian life.

Conflict can, therefore, be justified under certain conditions for some Christians, but not all.

Activities

1 Find these quotes in the Book of Matthew in the Bible and write them down. What do they suggest to Christians about conflicts, enemies and how to treat others?
   a Matthew 5: 9
   b Matthew 5: 44
   c Matthew 7: 12
   d Matthew 22: 39
   e Matthew 26: 52

2 In pairs, create a debate between a pacifist Christian and a Christian who believes in a just war. You might act it out, create a video, present it as a radio programme with an interviewer, or write it as a scene in a play.

3 If you were a Christian, would you be a pacifist or a just war Christian? Give reasons or examples to support your choice.

4 If you were asked to fight in a conflict, what conditions would you set down before you would be willing to risk your life and possibly kill others? List your own five conditions. (For example: 'The country I live in must be in danger' or 'I must have my family's agreement'.)

Our scientific power has outrun our spiritual power. We have guided missiles and misguided men.

● Martin Luther King was a Christian pacifist. Put his quote into your own words.

Getting technical

Just war a war that is regarded as just or morally acceptable.

Conscientious objector a person who refuses to take part in a war due to their conscience or beliefs.

61

Do religions cause conflict?

You might have heard people say that 'religions cause conflicts and suffering'. This section will help you to challenge this idea and make up your own mind about religions and conflict. Read the following discussion and discover your own views by answering the questions below it.

Clashes in Northern Ireland are an example, but is religion really causing the conflict here? Could other causes also be at play, like fear, political power, or revenge?

● Bomb explosion in Northern Ireland.

David: Religions! I don't know why people get involved with them! They cause so much conflict and suffering!

Rachel: I don't agree! I think Christianity does a lot of good. For me, it's basically saying that we should love God and love each other. And Abdul was telling me that the word 'Islam' can be translated as the word 'peace'. He says the Qur'an is full of quotes about looking after each other with kindness and love. I think we can get the wrong ideas from just watching the telly.

David: Yes, but what about the Protestants and Catholics in Northern Ireland? They're both Christian groups, but they've been fighting for decades! And what about the attack on the World Trade Centre in New York? That was done by Muslims wasn't it? How peaceful and loving was that?

Rachel: But if a Christian stabs someone or a Muslim steals something, you wouldn't say that's *because of their religion* would you? It's the person who is to blame. Holy books and beliefs don't hurt humans, people do!

David: But they might hurt someone *because* of what it says in their holy book.

Rachel: I don't know. I don't think any holy books say it's OK to kill people. Anyway, it depends on how you interpret it. Some people might read the books and get a totally different meaning from the words. Now, is the book responsible for those differences, or is it more to do with how we read it? I still think that it's people's choices that make wars and conflict, not the religions themselves!

David: So, if religions are not to blame for bad actions, surely they can't get the credit for the good actions either? If religions can help to create goodness in people, surely they can help to create the bad as well?

Activities

1. Give reasons why David might think religions cause conflict and suffering. Can you think of examples to support his views?

2. Do you agree that we 'get the wrong ideas' about religions from 'just watching the telly'? What images of Islam or Christianity do you see in the media (TV, newspapers, and so on)? Are the images unfair to the religion?

3. Explain how Rachel argues against David's examples of the 'World Trade Centre' and 'Northern Ireland'. Is this a convincing argument? Say why or why not.

4. Rachel argues that people are responsible for conflict, not religions themselves. Do you agree with her? Explain your answer.

5. How does David reply? What point do you think he is trying to make here?

6. Do you think religions do anything to stop conflict and suffering in the world? Give an example if you can.

7. Try continuing David and Rachel's conversation in writing or with a partner. What would Rachel say next in reply to David's last point, for example?

Extension Activity

8. Now that you have thought about Rachel and David's ideas, try to summarise your own views by writing a few sentences. (You might imagine someone has just asked you the question: 'Do religions cause conflict?' How would you reply now?) Make a class opinions chart with the heading 'Do religions cause conflict?' Stick it on the wall and display the class views on it. Add some illustrations, cartoons or pictures too!

9. Now check each other's opinions out. What were the general class feelings about the issue?

● How would you complete Rachel's comments?

Jihad

On 11 September 2001, two passenger planes were steered into the World Trade Centre towers in New York. The results were devastating. Both towers completely collapsed within the hour and over 3000 lives were lost. The world's media raced to investigate and communicate the causes: 'Muslim extremists' had struck against America. The word 'jihad' was suddenly very common on TV and in the newspapers. But what does it mean and has the media understood it properly? This section will help you to answer these questions.

To some, jihad simply means 'holy war'– a war that is fought by Muslims for religious reasons. The destruction of the World Trade Centre, it was sometimes reported, was an act of 'jihad'. However, the term 'jihad' can never be properly used to describe acts of terror. In fact, jihad has a much broader – and peaceful – meaning to it.

What does jihad mean?

Jihad is an Arabic word, and means 'struggling' or 'striving' to serve Allah (the Muslim word for God). There are two main types of jihad.

Greater jihad – this describes the striving of Muslims to follow the way of their religion (Islam) and to combat evil on a personal level. It involves Muslims' inner effort, courage and determination to be good and follow the commands of Allah. This is considered to be the 'greater' form of striving because a Muslim must conquer some very difficult enemies – their own weaknesses.

Lesser jihad – this describes the striving of Muslims to defend Islam and come to the aid of any fellow Muslim who is being attacked for practising Islam. The aim is to allow Muslims to practise Islam freely. Conflict is not allowed for reasons of hatred or revenge and all fighting must stop as soon as peace is possible.

Jihad is not an act of terror or violence against innocent people. It is the struggle to be a good Muslim and for the freedom to practise a peaceful religion that values all life.

● What do you struggle or strive for in yourself?

● Was this an act of jihad as the media sometimes claimed?

Getting technical

Jihad striving or struggling for the sake of Allah.

Muslim someone who believes in the religion of Islam.

Islam a religion that started about 1400 years ago in Saudi Arabia.

Activities

1. Why might some Muslims be upset or worried if newspapers call the destruction of the World Trade Centre an act of 'jihad'?

2. If you are not a Muslim, why might it be important for you to know what jihad does – and does not – mean?

3. What do you struggle or strive for in yourself? (Do you struggle to do homework or get out of bed on some mornings? Do you strive to conquer a fear you have?)

4. Why do you think greater jihad might be seen as more difficult than lesser jihad? Why is it 'greater'?

Extension Activity

5. Create a collage, picture, design, piece of music or poem called 'The struggle within'. Be imaginative and involve your feelings and ideas!

Not forgetting, but forgiving

It is easy for conflicts to escalate or spiral out of control. This section will help you to understand why this is and whether the 'conflict spiral' can be stopped.

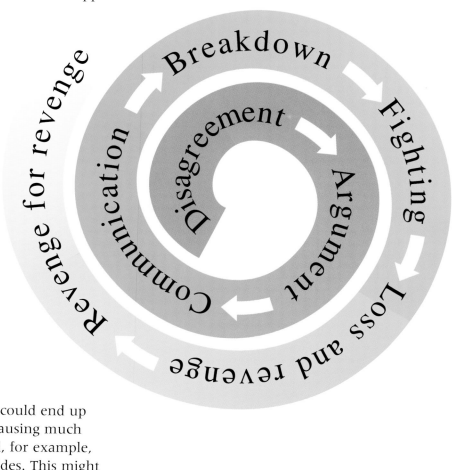

The conflict spiral

What starts as a minor disagreement could end up as a tragic disaster costing lives and causing much suffering. The disagreement may lead, for example, to a heated argument between two sides. This might cause both parties to stop talking to each other and encourage them to try to reach their goals through other means, such as violence or force. Side A may attack Side B, making them feel frightened or humiliated. Side B then takes revenge or attacks in self-defence, causing Side A to retaliate (fight back). And so it could continue.

Getting technical

Conflict spiral a conflict that is allowed to get worse and worse.

Activities

1. Can you think of any examples where this has happened in your own experience or in the world? Describe one example if you can.

2. What attitudes or problems can keep a spiral increasing?

3. What skills do people need to prevent a conflict spiral? At what point is it easiest to stop it escalating?

Yad Vashem

Sometimes people experience terrible suffering at the hands of others. As a result, the threat of conflict continuing for generations is very real. From 1933 to 1945, Jews living in many parts of Europe, especially Germany, were persecuted. During the Second World War (1939–45), 6 million Jews – one quarter of them children – were murdered under Nazi rule in the 'Holocaust' or 'Shoah'. Those who survived would never forget the deep sorrow and horror of those years. The pain, anger and desire for revenge that some Jews felt could have kept the violence going for decades afterwards.

Jews believe that it is very important to remember the Holocaust so that the dead are honoured and future generations are warned of the dangers of persecution. Yad Vashem is a special memorial area in Jerusalem, which is dedicated to all those who died. Many pilgrims visit it, particularly on the twenty-seventh day of the Jewish month of Nisan

think that there should be a national holiday in the UK in memory of the Holocaust victims.

However, not forgetting is quite different from not forgiving. It is a very important part of Jewish belief that the followers of Judaism should live by God's commandments and seek justice only through legal courts. Some Nazi war criminals were caught and sentenced, but many were not. For Jews, killing out of revenge or hatred is strictly forbidden and would not necessarily end the conflict or suffering. It is up to each Jew to try their best to forgive those who have caused them pain and suffering and leave God to judge them in the afterlife. Forgiving is a deeply challenging but central part of Jewish belief.

Getting technical

Conflict spiral a conflict that is allowed to get worse and worse.

● What does this sculpture at Dachau concentration camp suggest to you? What do you think the sculptor wanted people to think or feel when they saw it?

Yad Vasheem.

Getting technical

Retaliation fighting back in response to being attacked.

Persecution being treated cruelly because of race, religion or belief.

Yad Vashem a place in Jerusalem dedicated to the memory of those who died during the 'Shoah' or Holocaust.

Yom Hashoah Holocaust Remembrance Day; the day each year when Jews remember the suffering of Jews during the Holocaust.

Quote box

'To err is human, to forgive, divine.'
Alexander Pope, (1688–1744), English poet

Activities

1. Explain any connection you can see between the conflict spiral and the Jewish belief in forgiveness. In your opinion, how important is forgiveness in conflict resolution? Explain your answer.

2. Why might it be important to remember a past conflict?

3. Are there things that you could never forgive someone for doing? (A friend who let you down, a drink driver who injured a family member, or a thief who stole all your belongings, for example?) Would they have to accept responsibility for doing wrong to you or could you forgive them if they did not? Give examples to help explain your views.

4. In your own words, how would you define what 'forgiveness' actually means?

How can conflicts be resolved?

If you are involved in a conflict of some sort, what options might you have? This section will look at some different attitudes you could choose when dealing with a conflict and will focus on a Buddhist approach to the problem.

Here are ten possible attitudes or tactics that might be used in a conflict situation.

- Fight back
- Walk away
- Compromise
- Get help
- Forgive
- Apologise
- Postpone or delay
- Become angry
- Start a dialogue
- Ignore the problem

The Buddhist approach

Buddhists are very committed to the idea of 'ahimsa' or non-violence and try to treat all living creatures with compassion and kindness. They believe this for several reasons. First of all, they believe that violence will never offer a long-lasting solution to problems because violence just creates more anger, suffering and hatred. A second reason is due to their belief in 'interdependence'.

Getting technical

Dialogue a two-way conversation that often helps both sides in some way.
Compromise when both sides in a conflict make sacrifices so that an agreement can be reached.
Ahimsa a Buddhist word meaning 'non-violence'.
Compassion an attitude of love and kindness towards others.
Conflict resolution (finding) a solution to a conflict.

Activities

1. In small groups, prepare a short scene where a conflict occurs between all of you (an argument over 'which football team is best' or 'someone wrongly accused of stealing', for example).

2. Then choose one of the ten attitudes and plan out how your conflict would be affected by it. What would happen? Would the conflict end? Would a lasting resolution (solution) be achieved?

3. Now act out the conflict and your chosen resolution.

4. If you have time, try the same scene, but end it with a different attitude or combination of attitudes.

5. Are some attitudes always going to work? How could you tell which attitude to use in different conflict situations?

● Buddhists believe in finding non-violent solutions to conflict.

Interdependence

Interdependence means that all living beings rely on (are 'dependent on') each other for their existence. On one level, an individual certainly seems to be independent or separated from the world around them. However, on another level, individuals are connected to or dependent on their environment – and the living creatures within it – for their existence. For example, we need food, clothes, shelter, love, friendship and security if we are to be happy. Without other people, we would find it impossible to live a happy life.

Consequently, Buddhists do not really regard humans as being 'separate individuals', even though we might *appear* to be. All living creatures depend on other lives and our actions and attitudes should be kind and compassionate. To harm others is like harming ourselves.

This sounds wonderful, but of course it is not always easy. Tibetan Buddhists in particular have been strongly challenged in holding their belief in ahimsa. In 1950, the Chinese army invaded Tibet and China still rules over the Tibetan people. Over 1,000,000 Tibetans have died since the Chinese occupation – that is one in six of the entire Tibetan population. Staying non-violent and treating others with compassion can take enormous courage and strength.

● The Dalai Lama

> 'The only factor that can give you refuge or protection from the destructive effects of anger and hatred is your practice of tolerance and patience.'
>
> The Dalai Lama, world famous Tibetan Buddhist

What are 'tolerance' and 'patience' exactly, and how could they help in a conflict situation? Do you agree with the Dalai Lama?

Getting technical

Interdependence everything relies on everything else for its existence.

Activities

1. Put the Buddhist idea of 'interdependence' in your own words.

2. Do you agree with it? Give reasons for your answer.

3. Do you think 'ahimsa' means 'giving in to everything'? Give an example of making a change through non-violent methods.

Extension Activity

4. Can you discover:
   a. where Tibet is?
   b. some pictures or images of Tibetan Buddhists?
   c. a few key facts about the Dalai Lama?
   d. some websites that might tell you about Tibet and the Chinese occupation?

Case study – Martin Luther King: A way of Christian change

Martin Luther King (1929-68) was a Christian minister who felt that black people were being unfairly treated in America in the 1960s. He was determined to fight for equal rights for black people, and because of this his life was often threatened by white American racists. However, King was committed to the teachings of the Bible and did not believe that violence could solve conflict in the long run.

Influenced by the peaceful methods of Mahatma Gandhi, Martin Luther King used non-violent action to change things. For example, he organized and spoke at huge protest marches and encouraged black people to boycott bus companies that were racist. One of his most famous speeches is called the 'I have a dream' speech, when King told of his hopes for the future when black and white children could sit down together and feel equal and be friends.

Eventually, black people were given the vote in America, and more rights. King was assassinated on his hotel balcony by James Earl Ray in 1968.

Activities

1. Martin Luther King did not agree with other black leaders at the time (such as Malcolm X) who believed that sometimes violence is necessary to overcome an evil enemy. But is pacifism always right? Is it always practical? How can a person tell the difference between times when violence would work and when it wouldn't?

Getting technical

Boycott when a group of people stop buying products or supporting an organization/group in order to make them change.

Review and reflect

This chapter has been about conflict and conflict resolution. Here are some of the areas that you might have investigated.

- The different types and levels of conflict.
- The different possible causes of conflict.
- Whether conflict can be justified (from a Christian viewpoint).
- Whether religions – or people – cause conflict.
- What jihad does and does not mean (a Muslim view).
- The role of forgiveness in conflict resolution (and Yad Vashem).
- How conflicts might be prevented or stopped.

You have also learned some new vocabulary and developed your own ideas about complex and important issues. So how much have you learned? Try these challenges to give yourself an idea of your own progress.

● What might this child say to the soldier? How might the soldier reply?

Activities

1 In your own words, describe what the following words mean:

a conflict	**f** Yad Vashem
b conflict resolution	**g** conflict spiral
c pacifism	**h** forgiveness
d just war	**i** persecution
e jihad (greater and lesser)	**j** compromise
	k ahimsa.

2 In pairs or small groups, discuss the following opinions and answer the questions that follow them.

- 'It is always wrong to fight in a war if you are a Christian.' Give two different Christian views about this comment and add your own opinion.

- 'Religions just cause conflict in the world. If we did not have religions, we would not have religious wars.' Is this true? Do religions cause conflict or can they help resolve conflicts? Give at least two opinions.

3 Create a 'Peace Plan' for any two groups that are involved in a conflict. Include a list of guidelines (rules, attitudes) that each side needs to find a solution together. See if you can include the words 'forgiveness', 'compromise', 'tolerance' and 'dialogue'.

4 Give an example of 'being in conflict with yourself'. (For example, part of you may feel strongly about being vegetarian, but part of you might be desperately wanting a bacon sandwich.) How could you go about resolving the conflict within yourself? What advice could you give to someone in this situation?

5 Think back over the work you have done in this chapter. Pick at least four statements that you really agree with and two that you would like to improve upon.

- I participated (took part) in class discussions well.
- I listened to others carefully.
- I helped others.
- I spoke clearly and made myself understood.
- I gave reasons and examples to support my views.
- I developed my own ideas about 'conflict'.
- I understand more about 'conflict resolution'.
- I learned the meanings of at least four new words.
- I know more about religious views about conflict.
- I worked well outside of lessons.

How could you develop the two areas that you would like to improve? (Make a plan and act on it.)

Chapter 5

School linking: an introduction

Have you ever thought about the fact that your school is just one of millions around the world? Even the school nearest to you will not be exactly like yours. Every school is different and that is what this unit is about. The point of the 'school linking' part of the Citizenship course is to realize how you can learn from a school where you are not actually a pupil! Throughout this unit you will think about the following things:

A

Learn about...

- How we can all learn from people who are different to us.

- What your own school offers as a learning experience.

- What contrasting experiences schools in other parts of the world could offer.

- How to make and sustain links with another school.

- How to share what you have learned through school linking.

● Lesssons in an African school.

B

● A lesson at a school in the UK.

C

Activities

1. Write a list of things that you think all schools across the world have in common.

2. What is school for? Write a snappy quote summing up the purpose of school in 50 words or less.

◐ Playtime at a school in Africa.

'In the fight against poverty and crime, our weapon is education.'

Nelson Mandela

'The child with a good education flourishes. The child given a poor education lives with it for the rest of their life. How much talent and ability and potential do we waste? How many children never know not just the earning power of a good education, but the joy of art and culture and the stretching of imagination and horizons which true education brings? Poor education is a personal tragedy and national scandal.'

Tony Blair, Prime Minister, Labour Party conference, Brighton 2001

D

● Nelson Mandela.

F

● Tony Blair

E

● ICT in a British school

Getting technical

3 Look at the pictures above and on the opposite page. How do you think lessons in an African school are different to those in the UK? How do you think they are the same? List as many ways as you can.

Education the process by which we learn, and the end product of what we have learned.

4 Look at the quote from Nelson Mandela above. How do you think education can help in the fight against poverty and crime? Explain your answer fully, giving examples to support your opinions.

5 Look at the quote from Tony Blair. Do you agree that 'poor education is a personal tragedy and national scandal'? Give reasons for your answer.

Extension Activity

'Education is the great engine of personal development. It is through education that the daughter of a peasant can become a doctor, that the son of a mineworker can become the head of the mine, that the child of farm workers can become the president of a great nation.'
Nelson Mandela

6 Discuss this quote with somebody else in your class. What do each of you think the quote means? Are there any parts of it you disagree with? Write a paragraph explaining your reaction to this quote.

Where in the world?

In this section you will be given the opportunity to consider how you are already linked to people all over the world. You will need to record your findings in your books, but you will also need a copy of a world map which you can write on to show just how many countries you have links with.

Activities

1 Many of us have links with people who live in different places from ourselves. Think of a link you have with:
  a someone else who lives near you
  b someone else who lives in the United Kingdom
  c someone else who lives in a different part of Europe
  d someone else who lives on a different continent.

For each of the above, write who it is, where they live, and how you are linked. On your copy of the world map, using the key, mark on the places where these people live.

Activities

2 Even if we do not actually know people who live in different parts of the world, we are all dependant on people from other places in some way. Think of:
  e a place you have been on holiday
  f a country where tea or coffee is grown
  g a country where cocoa beans to make chocolate are grown
  h a country where something you are wearing was made (it usually tells you this on the label).

For each of the above, record this information in your book and mark on your map using the key.

Getting technical

NATO North Atlantic Treaty Organisation – this was set up after the Second World War in order to provide a defence alliance for its member countries.

Key

For Activity 1 answers, draw a small triangle △ and put the letter inside.

For Activity 2 answers, draw a small circle ○ and put the letter inside.

For Activity 3 answers, draw a small square ☐ and put the letter inside.

For Activity 4 answers, draw a small diamond ◇ and put the letter inside.

Activities

3 The United Kingdom itself has links with other parts of the world. These help the United Kingdom in areas like politics and economics. Political links help countries exist peacefully together. Economic links help countries trade with each other. Think of:

i a country in the European Union (EU)

j a country in the Commonwealth

k a country in NATO

l a country that is a member of the United Nations.

As before, record your answers in your book and also on your map.

When you record your answers in your book, make sure you explain your reasons for them. Remember to mark your map again.

Activities

4 Now think about links that may not exist yet, but which could be made. Think of:

m a country you would like to visit

n a different country from which you would like a pen-friend

o a country where the summer months are December, January and February

p a country where you think it is not compulsory for people of your age to go to school.

Getting technical

United Nations a world organistion which aims to promote international co-operation.

Politics matters to do with running or governing a country.

Economics matters to do with money and trading.

Beginning to make a link

We have thought about how our lives are enriched by an interest in and involvement with life in other countries. We have also thought about why it is important that we are all different. Now it is time to think about actually making a link with a school in another part of the world. You may already have some ideas about this. For example, you may wonder what it is like to have a long, hot Christmas holiday like in New Zealand or whether the teachers are allowed to cane pupils in other countries.

In other parts of the world, children have questions they would like to ask British school pupils – about their school life and about the United Kingdom as a whole.

We all form opinions of what other countries are like through reading about them and through images we see in the media. However, these images are often stereotypes. If we could talk to people about what their country is like, we would have a much clearer picture of it. Your school link will enable you to do this. There are some activities on pages 80–81, which will help you to think through your ideas before, during and after you have made your link.

Do you think these images (A to C) show a true picture of life in the United Kingdom? What three images would you choose to use?

How your school makes its link will depend on individual circumstances. But whomever the link is with, they will be interested in getting away from the stereotyped picture of the United Kingdom and learning about your perception of it.

Individuals within your link school will also be interested in you and your experience of life in the United Kingdom. They will want to know about the different communities you belong to and details of your daily life.

Activities

1. Complete this sentence with ten examples to show why it is a good thing we are all different. Think of some things that would not get done because you cannot or do not do them. You could make some of your examples amusing.

    'If everyone in the world was just the same as me…'

2. Make two lists to show what you like and dislike about living in the United Kingdom. An example has been done below.

    Likes
    We have a good health service.

    Dislikes
    The weather is not great.

Getting technical

Stereotype an image of something held in our minds, based on prejudices we have, rather than fact.

● A red telephone box.

● A beefeater.

● A Sunday roast.

Activities

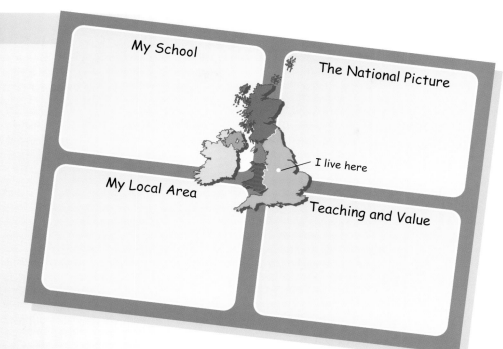

My School

The National Picture

I live here

My Local Area

Teaching and Value

1 Produce an A3 size poster that informs someone in your school about your life. Remember to include details about:

- Your school
  - your class
  - number of pupils and teachers
  - structure of the school day
  - curriculum
  - buildings/facilities
  - any other useful details about your school.

- Your local area
  - locate it on a map of the United Kingdom
  - local industries
  - local customs and food
  - any other interesting information about your local area.

- The national picture
  - the size of the country, including how big it is and how many people live in it
  - the government of your country
  - the different religions and cultural groups represented in your country
  - links with other countries in Europe and the Commonwealth.

- Teachings and values that are important to you
  - how you like to be treated
  - how you think we should treat other people
  - important lessons life has taught you
  - any proverbs or wise sayings you find helpful. For example, 'What goes around comes around'.

Use writing and pictures/photographs to make your work as interesting as possible. Your poster will be sent to your linking school, so make sure you keep a photocopy of it.

Extension Activity

2 Create your poster on the computer and e-mail it as an attachment to your partner school if the technology is available. Make sure you keep a copy of this as you will need it to use it in the future.

What can we learn from our partner school?

After you have made your link with your partner school, you need to look carefully at the information they send you. It is exciting to find out about other people and we can learn a lot about ourselves as we think about the similarities and differences between us.

We need to remember that there are likely to be many differences between your school and your partner school. This does not, however, make anyone 'better' or 'worse' than anyone else. Differences are good and we should accept that some things are different and not judge them.

Activities

1 Get out your photocopied poster from the previous activity. Your teacher will give you a similar poster produced by a child in your partner school. You are now going to analyse the information. Look first at the section called 'Your school'.

   a How many pupils attend your partner school? Which school is bigger?
   b Do you go to school on the same days of the week?
   c Who spends longer in school – you or your partner school's pupils?
   d Are there any subjects you both do?
   e Are there any subjects that your partner school studies and you do not?
   f Are there any subjects that you study and your partner school does not?
   g Why do you think there is a difference in your timetables?
   h How do your school's buildings and facilities compare with your partner school?
   i What other interesting facts have you learned about your partner school?
   j Now make a list of new questions you would like to ask about your partner school.

2 Look now at the section called 'Your local area'.

   a Which area is nearest the coast, yours or your partner school?
   b What are the local industries near your partner school? How are they similar to or different from the ones near you?
   c Do you think you would enjoy the local food? Why or why not?
   d What other interesting facts have you learned about your partner school's local area?
   e Now make a list of new questions you would like to ask about your partner school's local area.

3 Look now at the section called 'The national picture'.

   a How big is the country where your partner school is?
   b Who rules their country? How were they chosen? Is this the way your leaders are chosen?
   c What are the religions represented in the country? How are they similar to or different from the religions represented in the United Kingdom?
   d Does the country have links with any other countries? Is it linked to the United Kingdom at all?
   e Now make a list of new questions you would like to ask about your partner school's country.

Now you know some new facts about your partner school and country, think a bit more about the deeper lessons we can learn through our link by thinking about the beliefs and values people have. As you look at all the responses from your partner school, you should be able to build up a picture of what they consider to be essential in enabling people to live together peacefully.

Getting technical

Beliefs things that a person thinks are true.
Values principles that a person believes are right or wrong.

Activities

1. Look in the section on your partner school poster called 'Teachings and values that are important to you'. Choose five pieces of advice from your partner school that you think are the most helpful. Create a 'brick wall' picture in your book or as a display, and write these 5 pieces of advice on your wall.

2. Choose one of the teachings from your wall. Write a paragraph explaining how you could apply this in your daily life and why it is important to do so.

3. It would be very interesting to see what kind of community could be made by combining elements from your own life with that of a pupil in your partner school to create the 'ideal community'. What do you think your ideal community would be like? Describe it in at least one paragraph.

Nurturing and strengthening our link

Before we meet someone new we often wonder what they will be like. We may have pre-conceived ideas or stereotypes in our minds that are actually proved wrong when we get to know the person better.

Before you make your link

Activities

1. Write a list of five stereotypes about the United Kingdom. Now write a list of five stereotypes about your partner country.

2. Create a Vox Pop (this means 'voice of the people') of views about your partner country. Try to interview many different people, asking them to explain what they think of the country. You can either video or tape-record their responses. Make sure you ask their permission first. Possible questions could include 'can you locate country X on a map? 'What language do they speak there?'

During your link

Now that you have begun to get to know some pupils from another country, you can begin to assess how accurate your initial ideas were.

Activities

1. Create a class box of items connected to your partner country. It might include labels from food produced in the country, newspaper articles and photographs from holiday brochures. Every time you find an item bring it in, describe it to your class, then put it in the box.

2. Catch up with one person from your Vox Pop and update them with the new information you have discovered from your link school.

3. Keep a detailed diary of everything you do for a week. Ask a pupil in your partner school to do the same. E-mail or post these accounts to each other. Compare your results. How are your weeks similar and how are they different? Where would you rather be and why?

Tuesday 21 March

Got up early at 7.30am so I could have a shower and wash my hair before school. I enjoyed RE today as Miss Stewart got us to do role plays. Maths was hard but Miss Miley made me laugh then explained how to do the work. I did not enjoy English as I got told off for forgetting my homework. We got wet in games as it rained when we were playing hockey. At lunchtime, I went to the canteen with my friends Holly, Joe and Craig. I ate sandwiches and the others had pizza and salad.

After school I went home and my mum had made tea. In the evening I went to cadets where we learned how to read a map.

I went to bed at 9pm.

After your initial link

You have now learned a lot of information about a new country and a school in it. You will now know more about this place than most other people in your local area. It is your responsibility to share with others what you have learned to try to combat some of the stereotypical views people hold. There are many ways you can do this. For example, you could write an article for a local newspaper or take an assembly. One of the best things you could do is hold a special event, like a Link Day, designed to inform others about the reality of your link country.

Help box

Hosting a Link Day

Planning
Before you hold your event you need to think through the answers to these questions.

- When and where are you going to hold your event? For example, during the day or in an evening.
- Who are you going to invite? For example, your parents, local dignitaries or another class.
- Who are you going to need to help you? For example, your head teacher, your citizenship teacher, your food technology teacher.
- Is there any specific information you are going to need to ask your partner school for? For example, recipes for food from the country, music for their national anthem.
- What is going to be the format of the event? For example, people walking round to different activities, or people sitting and listening to a presentation, or a bit of both.
- What is the most important information about your partner country that you want to communicate to your community? For example, what stereotypes do you need to address? How are you going to share facts about the country and the values they hold?

Preparing
In order for your event to run smoothly you need to prepare carefully for the day. Some things will need to be done in advance and others on the day itself.

- What resources do you need? For example, posters, food, equipment.
- What rehearsals do you need to have? For example, drama rehearsal.
- How are you going to invite people and keep a record of who is coming? For example, specific invites, posters, an advert in a newspaper.
- Who is going to co-ordinate everything to make sure everything gets done? It is probably a good idea to have a teacher in overall charge of the event, but you might have a smaller committee who helps.
- Who is going to set up the room where you are holding the event? For example, the school staff, a group of volunteers.

Extension Activity

Write a report of your link day for your school magazine or even a local newspaper. Remember to explain what the purpose of the event was, say how you planned and prepared it, how it went and whether or not it achieved its purpose.

Case study – School linking

Brazil

In April 1998 four schools from Parana State in Brazil made links with four schools in the North West of England, from Bakewell in Derbyshire to Oldham in Lancashire. All eight schools were interested in sharing environmental education resources via the Internet. One of the goals was to stimulate the study of environmental issues among children, while promoting the use of IT as a source of learning.

Initially, the United Kingdom schools met to plan how they could share information and resources and to discuss environmental education issues to be included in the project. The teachers co-ordinating the link attended a school-linking seminar organized by the British Council.

Progress seemed slow at times because of communication problems. However the teachers were reassured as they realised that this is not uncommon. At one point the programme was delayed due to difficulties installing computers at the four Brazilian schools. The United Kingdom schools do not teach Portuguese, although one of the English teachers involved can speak some Portuguese and they are considering using BBC language tapes. In Brazil, an English language teacher works with the project teacher.

Current plans include going live with Internet homepages and developing projects between the schools. They plan to 'personalize' the link between pairs of schools to make closer ties now that the project is under way, while maintaining the support network of the local group.

Article taken from
http://www.wotw.org.uk/showcase/brazil.html

Activities

1. Look at the case study above.
   a What have the pupils learnt from their project?
   b What difficulties have the schools faced?
   c What have they done to try and combat the problems?
   d What plans do they have for the future?

Review and reflect

Your link with your partner school should be ongoing. You may even still be communicating with someone from your partner school when you are in your 50s! However, it is important to take time to reflect, at regular intervals, on what you are learning from your link. On the right are some helpful questions for you to consider.

Through your link you have been able to learn more about the values your partner school's country considers to be important. You have also had to reflect upon the values you hold.

Activities

1 **a** What is the most interesting thing you have learned through your link?
   b What surprised you the most?
   c Which stereotypes have been proved wrong?
   d Which stereotypes do you think are closest to the truth?
   e What do you think you have been able to teach your partner school about your school?
   f What do you think you have been able to teach your partner school about life in the United Kingdom?

Activities

2 Make a motivational poster for your partner school to display showing a value from the United Kingdom. Ask them to make a poster for you to display in your classroom. A motivational poster is one which inspires you to achieve more or think differently about the things you are learning. Your poster should inspire others to do better in their education, manners or behaviour.

3 Create a giant 'Wall of wisdom' in your classroom. Put values from the United Kingdom in one colour and values from your partner school country in another. Remember to try and apply the teachings that impress you in your own life.

Learning about your partner school's community might offer inspiration for a new way to deal with a problem in your own local community.

Activities

4 Think of a situation in your local community that needs changing. An example could the amount of grafitti in the local area, which needs to be cleaned off, and people need to be stopped from doing it. How can you apply what you have learned from you partner school to make changes in your own community?

If you expect respect be the first to SHOW IT

30 years from **now**, it won't **matter** what shoes you wore, how your hair looked, or the jeans you **bought**. What will matter is what you **learned** and how you **used** it.

● Some motivational posters

Chapter 6

Reviewing your evidence –
end of Key Stage 3 assessment

Learn about...

- What the end of Key Stage 3 assessment is.
- How you can gather a range of evidence for your assessment.

You have now reached the end of your Citizenship course at Key Stage 3. The way your school has organized your course will vary from the way another school organizes their Citizenship course.

You will have taken part in a vast range of activities, including working in class, working with others and taking part in community activities. Sometimes you will have undertaken traditional written work, but a lot of your work may have involved:

- discussions
- debate
- being involved in practical activities.

At the end of Key Stage 3 your teachers have to assess the progress you have made since Year 7. Unlike some other subjects, this assessment does not involve a formal test or writing answers to questions.

For Citizenship there is only one assessment statement. You are expected to have good knowledge of:

✓ topical events you have studied
✓ rights and responsibilities of citizens
✓ work of the voluntary sector
✓ different types of government
✓ how we provide public services
✓ how the criminal and legal system work
✓ how people get information
✓ how the media works
✓ how changes take place.

You should understand the importance of working with others.

Here are some examples of evidence you might have available to help in your assessment:

Traditional written notes or completed work

Display material

Records of events you have taken part in

Your school reports in Years 7, 8 and 9

Outside school club/activity records

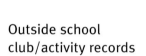

Your involvement in decision making within your school

Research undertaken on the Internet

Photo or video evidence of debates or visits

Notes in your school diary or contact book

Awards/certificates given at school

School 'press cuttings' about Citizenship events

Copies of letters written to individuals and their replies

ICT work/records

During the past three years you will have undertaken a vast range of activities. They may not all have been labelled 'Citizenship'. However, all the subjects you are taught at Key Stage 3 contain elements of Citizenship.

How does your experience measure up?

Activities

1 Complete a grid sheet based upon what you are expected to learn from Citizenship (see the checklist on p84) and the evidence you might have available.

Key Stage 3 Citizenship	Evidence
• Study topical events	• Help maintain the current events notice board/display for three weeks
•	•
•	•

2 Think about the things you liked best about Citizenship and those you least liked. Can you draw any conclusion about what you liked and disliked?

Presenting your evidence

A portfolio of evidence

Many of us keep a scrapbook or photo album to record and remember things that are important to us.

In recent years the government has encouraged students to maintain Records of Achievement, now called Progress Files, where you keep a record of your educational progress.

One way of keeping your Citizenship work is to create a Citizenship Progress File.

Evidence comes in a variety of forms. It does not all have to be written down and checked by your teacher.

As your Citizenship course develops, your file could become overwhelmed with 'evidence', so one of the skills you need to develop is the ability to decide which pieces of evidence are most important. A badly organized, bulky Progress File will not help you gain the assessment you would like. Remember, you want to show that you have undertaken a range of activities, that you have worked with others, and have been involved with the local community.

Remember that if you want to include personal items, it is best to keep only a photocopy in your Progress File so that the originals are kept safely at home.

● A student and teacher discuss Citizenship evidence.

Your portfolio

Have you added your views that show you have opinions about your Citizenship work?

Does it contain a range of evidence?

Have you reviewed the evidence so that it is not too bulky?

Does it have something from each year?

Does it show how you think you have made progress?

Does it involve activities inside and outside school?

Does it show you have worked with others?

Tip Keep a list at the back of the Progress File of all your evidence and mark the evidence you kept in the file with a special symbol.

Some evidence will relate to your work with others so it will not always be possible for every member of the group to have the evidence. In this case, just write a note in your file of who is holding what evidence.

Activities

1. A progress File can be organized in a variety of ways:
   a date order
   b by subjects/teachers delivering Citizenship
   c by type of activity.

   How would you organize a Citizenship Progress File? Give reasons for your choices.

2. The opening pages of the Progress File could be your thoughts about the Citizenship course you have followed. What would you write? What have you learned and gained from the course?

Getting involved and working with others

Active Citizenship is not about working alone and doing research. It is about getting involved, understanding issues, and working with others.

A major part of your Key Stage 3 Citizenship course will have involved you getting 'active' – being an 'active citizen'.

How were you an active citizen?

Did you:

Work as a member of a team

Take part in discussions or debates

Take on different roles within a team

Stand for election for the School Council

Work with a range of people from within your school: teachers, teaching assistants, older students, younger students, administration staff, caretakers, parents, governors, and so on

Getting involved and working with others means you have to use skills different from the ones you would use if you worked on your own. Planning has to take place, you have to work to timescales, you have to help each other and sometimes you have to take instructions from other people and do things you really do not want to do.

In your portfolio, what would you list as the ways you got involved at school?

How did you get involved in your local community?

Citizenship is not always about doing new things. It is also about recognising that what you do already is a part of being an active citizen.

To help your assessment, you may need to write a short record of your involvement in the community and ask your parents or group leader to sign it.

You may be asked to give a talk to your group or in a one-to-one with your teacher outlining your involvement with the local community.

Assessment at Key Stage 3 is not just a checklist of evidence written down and contained in a file. You and your fellow students may be actively involved in assessing each other's work.

You will listen to talks by fellow students, take part in debates and work with others in groups and teams. You will be involved in deciding how you assess fellow students.

What do you think are the important points for assessing Citizenship when someone is giving a talk? Think about:

Quality of research, style of presentation, visual aids, structure of talk, opportunity for questions, humour, ability to hold people's attention, strength of opinion, ability to persuade, keeping to time.

Is there anything else you could add? In what order would you place them all? Are some far more important than others?

Voluntary work

Helping recycling schemes

Visiting an elderly relative

Helping out at home

Belonging to a club or voluntary group, for example, football or the Scouts

1. Write an account of how you got involved in your school or local community. What did you most enjoy and least enjoy about this involvement?

2. Working with others, complete the following checklist, based on your involvement as a member of a group.

The task the group was completing:

_____
_____
_____

How/who decided what should be done?

_____
_____
_____

What role did you play?

_____
_____
_____

What skills did you have to use?

_____
_____
_____

What are the benefits and drawbacks of working as a team?

_____
_____
_____

What problems did you encounter and how did you overcome them?

_____
_____
_____

How did this activity improve your Citizenship understanding?

_____
_____
_____

Events and projects

Sometimes your Citizenship course has involved you in working on your own or with others for a considerable length of time to complete a task.

This type of activity or event means you have to develop a wide range of skills: sometimes just listening, observing others or being part of an audience. On these occasions, you could make your own contributions better by making judgements about the performance of others.

● Students drawing attention to the issue of fair trade.

● Students working with police in their school.

Some schools organize special events or activities as part of their Citizenship courses. This could involve the whole class or year group spending a whole day on Citizenship.

What skills are needed to organize such an event?

You and your class are set the task of organizing a half-day conference for your whole year group of 200 students. The theme is 'You and the law'.

What questions do you need to consider when planning this event?

Can you do it all on your own or do you need staff help?

How do you sort out timings? Are there any breaks?

How much space do you have?

How does everyone know what is happening and what to do?

Does the group of 200 stay together for the whole session?

How do you make sure there are different types of presentations

How does working in a team develop your Citizenship skills?

Who writes the letter explaining the event to parents?

Who do you invite to speak, make presentations or sit on a panel of speakers?

How does the audience get involved?

How do you know if the event was successful or if a particular part was more popular than others?

Map labels: Playcourt, Grass, Gardens, Playcourt, Stream, Playing Field, Main Hall, Classrooms, Grass, Gardens, Classrooms, Classrooms, Car park, Car park, Caretaker, Grass, Main gate

Activities

1. Having studied the points about the 'You and the law' event, outline how you would organize such an event at your school.

2. Your group has been asked to organize an evening at your school for parents to inform them about the Key Stage 3 Citizenship programme you have followed. How would you organize such an event?

Community activity and course review

Getting out and about is a vital part of your Citizenship course. Citizenship is about you and your local community, the society we live in, and how we are a part of an interdependent world.

Some of the work you have undertaken will be based in your local community and this should be reflected in your Progress File.

What local places do you think are suitable to visit as part of a Citizenship course?

How do you get the best out of these visits?

Have you done some background research?
Have you prepared some questions to ask?
How will you record the event – photographs, video, an article for the local press?
What do you expect from the visit? How are you expected to behave and react?
How do you find out more about your local community?

Who is the weakest link?

Can you answer these questions?

1 Who is your local MP?

10 How large is the catchment area of your school?

2 Where are the offices of your local council?

9 Identify five services provided by your local council.

3 How do you contact the local Citizens Advice Bureau?

8 What local newspapers are available?

4 Where are the local courts?

7 What is the name of your local councillor?

5 Can you name five local community groups for young people?

6 Who is the largest local employer?

Don't know the answers? How and where do you get help?

- local council
- school office
- parents
- friends
- local websites.

Citizenship is not about knowing all the answers, but knowing where to start to find the answers and having the confidence to start looking and asking.

Your file should include some evidence of your involvement with the local community.

● Gordon Brown supporting Barclays Bank new futures Citizenship initiative.

Review of the course

Key Stage 3 Citizenship is now drawing to a close. What impact has it made on you?

✓ Do you know more things?
✓ Are you more confident about working with others?
✓ Do you know more about your local community, society and the world as a whole?
✓ Has the course enabled you to develop your ICT skills and use them to produce a variety of different types of work?
✓ If you do not know the answers to everything, do you know where to start looking?
✓ Are you aware that sometimes issues are very complex and not simple to solve?

✓ Has the course helped you to understand that individuals and groups can make a difference and that as well as rights we have responsibilities?
✓ How would you describe the progress you have made in Citizenship at KS3?

If you can tick most things on this checklist, you are an active, not a passive, citizen.

Activities

1. Design a leaflet for Year 6 pupils coming to your school. The aim of the leaflet is to explain what a Citizenship course is like. Using ICT, design a two-sided A4 leaflet.

2. How would you describe the progress you have made in Citizenship at KS3?

Index